DIALOGUES
WITH BOULEZ

Rocco Di Pietro

The Scarecrow Press, Inc.
Lanham, Maryland, and London
2001

SCARECROW PRESS, INC.

Published in the United States of America
by Scarecrow Press, Inc.
4720 Boston Way, Lanham, Maryland 20706
www.scarecrowpress.com

4 Pleydell Gardens, Folkestone
Kent CT 20 2DN, England

British Library Cataloguing in Publication Information Available

Library of Congress Cataloging-in-Publication Data

Di Pietro, Rocco
  Dialogues with Boulez / Rocco Di Pietro.
    p. cm.
  Includes bibliographical references (p.) and index.
  ISBN 0-8108-3932-6 (alk. paper)
  1. Boulez, Pierre, 1925– —Interviews. 2. Composers—France—Interviews. I. Title.

ML410.B773 A5 2001
780'.92—dc21   00-061935

∞™ The paper used in this publication meets the minimum requirements of
American National Standard for Information Sciences—Permanence of Paper
for Printed Library Materials, ANSI/NISO Z39.48-1992. Manufactured in the
United States of America.

CONTENTS

ABOUT THE AUTHOR

Rocco Di Pietro is a composer-pianist, writer, and habilitationist. He works both as a social worker and as an interdisciplinary lecturer in the humanities for Columbus State College. His other books include *Musician without Notes,* a collection of writings and essays; *The Normal Exception: Life Stories of Incarcerated Men and Women* from *The Prison Dirges* cycle; and the monograph *Menocchio: A New Peasant Consciousness.* His Web site can be viewed at roccodi.freeyellow.com.

FOREWORD

In these fascinating dialogues, Pierre Boulez speaks a lot about developments and trajectories, and what he says helps us understand the course his creative life has taken, from the impulsive musical snapshots of his early youth to the long continuities with which he has been increasingly occupied since the mid-1960s. His commitment to the modernist spirit remains as intense as it was when he emerged as a firebrand of a composer more than half a century ago. He is, too, still critical of the modernist pioneers when they return to forms from the past, as Igor Stravinsky did in *Oedipus Rex* and Arnold Schoenberg did in certain of his twelve-note compositions. But the imperative to develop and extend a truly contemporary musical language has been joined by a wish to emulate the largeness music achieved at the end of the romantic era—in Richard Wagner's later operas and in the symphonies of Gustav Mahler, to cite two examples to which Boulez often returns. This is the task he has set for himself: to create works of similar scope, of similar richness in sound, expression, and form, without returning to gestures and harmonic systems that have lost their living intensity—to create grandeur, power, and mystery, all without irony.

Boulez is severe not only about Stravinsky and Schoenberg but about many of his contemporaries. One measure of the trust his interlocutors won from him is in the freedom and trenchancy with which he talks about John Cage, Karlheinz Stockhausen, and others. His criticisms are thoroughly based on his high ideals. Music, in his view, cannot be ill considered: it demands the utmost stretching of technical mastery and a full knowledge of the classics in addition to a lively imagination and a crucial ability to curve momentary insights and discoveries into the texture of the piece. These strictures are, of course, not only for others. Where he has found his own works lacking in expertise or control, he has withdrawn or revised them. Where he has found himself unable, for the moment, to proceed, he has waited—often for decades—before completing a project.

By the time these conversations were recorded, in the late 1990s, Boulez had long been a commanding figure. Stravinsky had recognized *Le Marteau sans maître* as a masterpiece more than forty years earlier, and, after some slack periods, the composer of that work had returned to active strength: *Sur Incises* for three pianos and six percussionists, *Notations VII* for large orchestra, and *Anthèmes II* for electronically modulated violin are among the recent works he talks about here. He was also—and this touches the circumstances of these encounters as much as their subject matter—enjoying new opportunities and acclaim as a conductor, revisiting his favorite twentieth-century repertory with the great orchestras of the world.

Yet the man who emerges from these pages is private. Confronted by positions sometimes distant from his own, Boulez opens himself as much as he dodges. And the book draws us close not only to the substance of his thinking but to his style, for the text captures, as few other Boulez interviews do, the forcefulness and the uncertainty in the rhythms of his speaking voice.

Paul Griffiths

PREFACE

I was one of those "failed composers," in the underground, Pierre Boulez had once remarked on. Now I was standing face to face with him, backstage at Orchestra Hall, in Chicago.

My path and life had taken several turns on the road of the creative life. Like a traveler, I had crossed various disciplines' boundaries and had mutated to the point where I sometimes could no longer recognize what I had become. Standing there looking at this man, I realized how very different our lives have been.

Actually, Boulez was once a former fire source of my youth, who had been relegated to the status of a failed god of a modernism that had gone underground. Most of the artists I have admired have wrestled with some sort of ambitious project that has escaped them—Alberto Giacometti and Francis Bacon, to name only two. In my mind now, I realized that we both had something in common. Through these different "failures," we were both fellow travelers in the creative imagination. Yet, the difference between us somehow felt important. Looking at him, I felt that he seemed frozen, immobile, becoming ever deeper.

Boulez was what I once admired in a composer, in the naïveté of my youth. In fact, he was the exemplar of what I felt had been denied to me. I had taken Stravinsky's advice and avoided the university, going directly underground, hoping one day to emerge. Unable to turn a quick million, I thought I had remained in the underground far too long. I was unable to become what I wanted to be and was forced to become who I am. This Nietzschean lesson of "become who you are" was a hard one. I scrutinized Boulez's face and wondered whether Boulez—in becoming who he wanted to be, by his own admission, by being in the right place at the right time, by an accident, in other words—had become who he really is.

Standing next to him I thought of Michel Foucault and questioned him on Georges Bataille. I felt a strange sense of power—not his, but my own power of having individuated. Boulez seemed vulnerable, a human being after all.

He looked at me for a long time, returning my gaze. He reminded me of my father; he is the same age. Both men are emotional underneath an outward appearance of discipline. Both men have that hardened Mediterranean face punctuated by laughter. When I listen to the tapes of our conversations, I am still struck by the amount of laughter they contain.

As I thought about where this meeting with Pierre Boulez was going, I knew that I had put the search for the fathers behind me. I could now see clearly that what Bruno Maderna told me years ago was true: "Most of what you read about Boulez in the press is false." In Cleveland at a preconcert discussion, Boulez fielded a question from the audience about one of these myths that persists. His answer was telling: "I am not a monk, you know, not at all." In New York amid all the flurry of his seventy-fifth birthday year, the *New York Times* admitted that while the reputation of polemical firebrand still followed him, the myths surrounding him were finally being revealed for what they were.

Here in Chicago my thoughts returned to the unforeseeable nature of what was happening backstage while I was talking to
Boulez. This meeting, after so many years, was an accident. I realized that I would have to question this man in an attempt to find
out what had happened to modernism. I knew almost immediately
that I would do this without polemic. I was interested in asking
questions, and although I admired this man now as a fellow traveler, I was not crazed with envy for what he had become.

After that, Boulez turned down my attempts to question him on
several occasions, as he turned down a half dozen requests for interviews in the Chicago area. It was only through Fran Huscher's
insistence that I got the interview at all. On that day another unforeseen problem had arisen, as he ate lunch with his assistant
Hans backstage, between recording sessions of the Varèse cycle he
was taping with the Chicago Symphony. He waved us off, saying
no; we went in anyway, and I fired off my first question, apologizing for asking such a difficult question while he was eating lunch.
He listened and burst into laughter, apologizing that unforeseen
difficulties had required him to change his plans. We agreed I
could stay for ten minutes. I turned on the recorder and asked him
the single most intense question I had prepared, actually five questions in one long paragraph.

Later, after I left, he told the program annotator that he liked my
question, and I would be invited back. At our first sessions Boulez
would simply pick and choose what part of my questions he felt
like addressing. Soon I started paring down my questions, as this
manner puzzled me. I discovered that this was an example of an
accident that happens once and is at the heart of Boulez's approach
to the art of the organic process. From this point on, the whole interview process would proceed with this éclat. Accidents happen
once but over time continually come your way; you pick and
choose to see whether they can give you something you need.

As I gained his trust, Boulez became comfortable with the conversational format that was developing. Boulez is very conversational and in many ways an informal speaker. He was never interested, in any case, in the one-line type of questions that journalists ask.

A piecemeal approach gradually unfolded that was based on circumstances that became a trajectory à la Boulez that led into unforeseen byways.

I organized the material for a second time into a loose topical format for the journal *21st Century Music* in California, which published our talks serially over four years. Later, I would schedule sessions with Boulez in both Chicago and Cleveland to set up follow-up questions to clarify some of the things Boulez did not answer the first time around.

I then reorganized all the material for a third time, reformatting the talks into three chapters with topical subdivisions for this book.

The idea that the initial interview had turned into a conversation and then mutated into a dialogue was going to be a bit of a problem to pull off. A dialogue is, after all, a conversation in literary form. Mind you, the problem was not with Boulez or me. Boulez always treated me as an equal with complete autonomy. In fact, a kind of shop talk between two composers developed rapidly. No, the trouble would come in presenting these dialogues for publication.

The pressure from editors to turn these conversations that became dialogue into a so-called straight or journalistic interview was very real. It required a lot of resistance, because it would have ruined the organic process that Boulez and I came to agree on.

I realized it would be hard to convince editors, who were using "science" as their yardstick, that a so-called literary approach to a dialogue could in fact give the raw data scholars were looking for. When I questioned scientist friends in other fields, they said they

could not understand what I meant since for them science is about gathering raw data from a source and not the other way around! Boulez was my source, and this project was in a way multicultural, with the Atlantic Ocean between Chicago, where the interviews mostly took place, and Paris, where Boulez always returned.

I pondered why today's world leaves so little room for dialogue. Publishers are against it generally—it doesn't sell. A dialogue implies a fluid give and take that is at best difficult for a world so compartmentalized and noisy. Specialists in every field are often unable to have a conversation with one another. David Bohm, the physicist, once said that scientists were too committed to their own views to be able to have a dialogue with each other.

Yet the scholarly tradition is not necessarily the intellectual tradition. Scholars are interested in information; intellectuals, it seems, are concerned with products. A dialogue is a place where sometimes the questions are as interesting as the answers.

Furthermore, our educational system is committed to the consumption of information and not necessarily to critical evaluation of that information that a dialogue may imply. This may be, as some have said, because the educational system is not set up for debate or dialogue. True, it brings out ideas as well as information, but the information that may come up in a dialogue could be information that you don't want, especially if the ideas are disturbing. This could force you to think dialectically, rather than to simply process information. "To be confronted with the challenge for change may be an area our educational system is not set up for," according to John Scoville, my colleague at Columbus State College, who from time to time sat in on these talks.

Early on in these conversations with Boulez, I sent out to potential editors bits of the dialogue transcribed directly from the tape recorder in the roughest format imaginable, just to test the waters I have been discussing concerning dialogue here. Given the

aforementioned ideas, it does not take much effort to imagine the results. Yet, once in a while a letter came back that spoke about the content of our project and not about the format, which caught our attention. This little test to weed out the uninterested was useful, and Boulez and I agreed that we should wait until I found a publisher "that would allow us to be ourselves." I found that editor in Ann Basart of Fallen Leaf Press and was very grateful. Later Scarecrow Press came along, and Shirley Lambert picked up where Ann and I left off, after Ann had retired.

As far as the text is concerned, instead of footnoting, I decided to preface certain sections. This was done to help the reader understand where Boulez has stood on an issue in the past and where he stands today, putting things into a larger perspective. This format also helps frame the longer questions with the necessary background material to help sharpen the dialogues' context by putting them into focus.

I added a bibliography to help the reader understand where some of the essential source material could be found on both the questions and the answers of this dialogue.

Since famous people give many interviews, they inevitably repeat themselves, sometimes with stock answers. If I happened to discover where Boulez might have said something similar before, I took the trouble to include it in the bibliography.

In looking over these talks, I found that Boulez comes back to several essential ideas on more than one occasion. In fact, by speaking about one thing, Boulez often illuminates his own thoughts on another. For example, in speaking about Cage and Chance, Boulez outlines several key ideas—namely, "responsibility," "tools," and "values"—as important to his philosophy of what it means for him to be an artist. In speaking of Stockhausen, he discusses his own concept of the "organic form" and how he is against what he calls the idea of building a cupboard

that is so inflexible it has to be filled with content that is watered down. He is clearly against the formula and what he calls a "theocratic vision" of creativity.

Once again, for Boulez the idea of the accident is very important. He takes great pains to distinguish just what he means by chance as compared to Cage's indeterminacy. He, in fact, describes the painter Francis Bacon's method of working with chance as almost identical to his own.

I was struck by how Boulez's mind works in pairs of opposites that often took these dialogues down some very interesting paths indeed. During one session, he told me that everyone is always looking for the meaning of whatever situation they happen to be in; that, in fact, they think they have found the right understanding, but in fact most situations in life are made up of misunderstandings. For Boulez, the misunderstanding is more important "for the creative person" than the right understanding, because, like the accident, it might give you something that you need. Lastly, in the summation question, Boulez sums up his entire philosophy of life when he answers in the language of physics and calls attention to the idea that his life has been like a spiral, with lots of accidents, that is never ending, but with some final end object tacked on to give it some momentary definition. He mentions Marcel Proust, as he does throughout these talks, as the artist whose concepts of creativity have been the closest to his own.

ACKNOWLEDGMENTS

First and foremost to Juli Douglass Gillespie for the first meeting with Boulez. To Robert Bracken and Polly Hill Valenzuela for setting up the next meeting and to Fran Huscher for making it happen. To Seneve Carlino and Phillip Huscher of the Chicago Symphony and Peter Laki of the Cleveland Orchestra. To Rob and Cy Griffith in Chicago, to Astrid Schirmer in Paris, and to Olivier Brossard in New York.

For work on the first writings of the manuscript, to Richard Nelson Peszka and Todd Harvey. For work on the second writing of the manuscript, to Mark Alburger of *21st Century Music* and Marie Bersom. For work on the third writing of the manuscript, to Aaron Smith, who reformatted the entire book onto disk, and to Barbara Adams, who converted the format from PC to Mac.

To John Scoville, whose friendship and insightful conversation have been invaluable. To Ann Basart of Fallen Leaf Press.

To the Paul Sacher Foundation for use of Boulez's manuscripts; to the Kittredge Fund and the Ludwig Vogelstein Foundation for financial assistance.

For reading drafts of the manuscript, to Bette Burgoyne, George Borelli, Bruno Di Pietro, Lukas Foss, Paul Griffiths, Russell Link, Tobias Schneebaum, Frances Marie Uitti, Jan Williams, and Natalie (Zemon) Davis.

Finally, to Rocco Di Pietro (Sr.), Pasquale Cimini, Delphine de Luna, John Di Pietro, and Nancy Cimini–Di Pietro.

I

COMPOSITION AND IMAGINATION

Phillip Huscher, writing in the program book of the Chicago Symphony Orchestra, describes Boulez's process of composition as follows:

> An idea in one piece often grows into another composition altogether, works continually evolve and are expanded, amplified, and revised over time. Boulez's output resembles a sizeable extended family. Mahler is the best parallel from an earlier time: his first four Symphonies and the "Wunderhorn Songs" are all interrelated, mutually illuminating works. Each of Boulez's scores is a component in a magnum opus in progress.

Boulez himself described this process when he said, "As long as my ideas have not exhausted every possibility of proliferation, they stay in my mind....The different works that I write are basically no more than different facets of a single central work, with a central concept."

I told Boulez that what strikes me about his oeuvre is its consistency over the years. Even during his tenure as music director of the

New York Philharmonic, one was struck by the steady flow of work that resulted. A rhythm of composing seems to have been set in place early on, and he must have realized that this flow or rhythm was congenial to his native self. However, somewhere he must have asked himself, "What else will I do with my time?" For example, Stravinsky composed about three hours a day, the rest of his time being taken up with various other tasks.

At one point it was reported that Boulez does not compose anymore. Even now, one hears from people that Boulez has not written anything new; he just reworks old material.

Years ago, Bruno Maderna told me not to believe anything that was written in the press about Boulez because none of it was true. In fact, he said, "Boulez is always working, always composing; the misunderstanding comes from the *way* he works." And then Maderna explained: "The way of Boulez is to take two weeks (for example) and think about one or two notes of the viola part in a large score, to make sure they are exactly the notes he wanted (where and how placed in the score) down to the last detail of how it is to be played." If this is true, it is amazing how prolific he has been. Perhaps the confusion has something to do with artists like Picasso or Stockhausen, who so rapidly create such an enormous quantity of new and varied work. That approach perpetuates the myth that the artist must be a producer of constantly new and dazzling works and that anything less is indicative of creative decline.

DI PIETRO: Today, Stockhausen has changed. He certainly seems to regard composition as one process, one work. It seems to me that you have always thought this way (I am thinking of Wagner). Beyond that, this approach of regarding problems of the entire oeuvre is a fundamentally different way of thinking, of conceiving music, than the one-work-at-a-time inspiration myth of artists portrayed in, say, Hollywood cinema. Even a painter like

Jackson Pollock succumbed to the fear that he might be washed up as an artist if he passed even so brief a period as six months without painting. With all this in mind, how is *Notations* coming along?

BOULEZ: Well, yes, this is the current problem of *Notations* and even more of *Visage nuptial*. It's true that I think about the work and the problems that the work itself proposes, for a long time. Certainly Maderna knew this. With the *Visage* it is a question of my first attempts being naïve or premature because my experience of writing for the instruments of the orchestra was limited, and this contributed to my not being able to formulate my ideas completely. It resulted in my putting the work aside and taking it up later after I had gained the experience of working with the orchestra. There are many ways of exciting the imagination and no single way when it comes to artistic creation. Of course, I have composed works that have been more or less straightforward that have not been subject to this process of the labyrinth, but for the most part I have been involved in the larger perspective of the process of the entire oeuvre, as you called it. This does not mean that works are never finished but that it may take twenty years to find solutions to the problems the work itself has proposed is very real for me. I think the most interesting example I can give is the case of Proust, in which I find a model for the kind of thing we are talking about—I mean the work being one long process throughout life. In the *Recherche du temps*, you find that Proust gives one character a particular theme or motif, only to find that the motif has been taken up much later by another character and entirely transformed, even if it is several volumes later. I was inspired by this in my own work *Notations*, where a seed from a piano piece is transformed and developed thirty years later into a gardenlike expansion of the orchestral *Notations*. This process of growth is very much like Proust, which I

found to be very interesting as a model for my own evolution and perhaps the closest of anyone to my own way of working.

DI PIETRO: So if I understand you, you yourself are actually the ground of this garden which needs to be worked—in this case the understanding of the orchestra which has grown incalculably since the 1950s—before the ideas or seeds, planted earlier, could actually bear fruit?

BOULEZ: Yes, certainly.

DI PIETRO: But only when the garden is ready.

BOULEZ: Of course, you have to prepare the ground, so to speak.

DI PIETRO: The image of an "orderly anarchist" is for me very close to that of a master gardener; I know that you have thought of yourself more in terms of a gardener—pruning, trimming, guiding the anarchy of creation. . . .

BOULEZ: With *Notations* I wanted to put my orchestral experience into a work where I had nothing to compose, but only ideas to work on, originally very short pieces for piano, reexamined after more than thirty years and developed for orchestra, as Berio would say, of "transcription." I read around the same time that in some Egyptian tombs they found corn seeds and put them in water and then in the earth, originally as an offering to the Gods, and the seed preserved after centuries produced again—not that I am comparing myself to any ancient Egyptian. However, I think that's a little bit of what happened here: the seeds were there far away, and then I began to conceive of these seeds as something for new development. So, of course, if you are involved in this kind of

process of composition of which we have been speaking, there will naturally be misunderstandings. For me the idea of one work at a time is a little superficial, since one's whole being is taken up with composition, not on every level at once, of course, but over time.

DI PIETRO: I was struck by several remarks of yours in the last essay of *Orientations* (a speech, I believe, upon receiving an award). The first was when you said "a large element of unconsciousness is needed to persevere along a path dictated by circumstances." Then you thanked the audience for "rewarding your gifts as a Sleepwalker." You had prefaced these comments with the idea that research (for you) is like hunger: "it cannot be satisfied once and for all." So, "The Hunger of the Sleepwalker," where the sleeper may engage in a variety of more or less coherent activities. These are extraordinary images that verge on the mystical. How can one balance the need to protect the unconscious aspect of creative life, with the conscious—let's say, "more rational"—forces of our everyday life? In other words, how do you do it? Is it a matter of what Maderna called "finding the *confidence* to just write the music down, since the music has always already existed"?

BOULEZ: Well, when I think of myself as a composer, there are two things in me: the side of the performer and the side of the composer. That's the same person, of course. But the approach is not exactly the same because, even when I conduct my own works I have some distance with them, not at all like when you are composing. As a composer, yes, you have to be at the same time adventurous, so you don't know what you will discover; I mean, you are on the path of a discovery and you know it. And you go about this in various ways. For instance, imitation or absorption is one way. You hear something. Or if you see something—a painting; or if you read a book, especially when you are

in an overlapping configuration or discipline which is not musical at all. Like painting, for example; suddenly you see someone's work who has found a solution to the problem, and it may be that you can say, "Oh, for my problem that can also apply." Of course, you have to transcend that, to find your own solution. It can provoke a solution. That's what I call not so much imitation, really, but absorption. Another way is the technical approach, which can also be quite useful, because when you are thinking of something you have a goal. Of course, at first it is still quite vague, but you have a goal nonetheless. You say to yourself, "I don't know how to reach that." At that point you might make some kind of exercise—a composition exercise. That will help you to find, perhaps, the solution to the problem you are thinking about, although it is still quite detached. At this point you are concentrating on a kind of technical problem, and then, suddenly, the ideas of the problem will coincide with what you want to express! So, you see, there are many ways of exciting the imagination; the sound can excite the imagination, without any other notion, for instance. Or, in a very abstract way sometimes, the idea of the form can excite our imagination. Then, that's exactly the contrary. When you have sound as the source of inspiration or the source of expression, you have to organize that in a way that the sound is not the only material. This material should be organized by some structure. And then, again on the contrary, sometimes when you think, directly, of the structure, you have to organize the sound to make it visual in the score and audible to the ear.

DI PIETRO: Could you tell me more about the "sleepwalker" comment you made at the end of that speech you gave in Munich upon receiving the Siemans prize? How is the image of the sleepwalker aligned with research as hunger?

BOULEZ: Well, one is never sure what you are doing, and I think even discoveries in science are something which is very intuitive. Sometimes you find something quite surprisingly; you may have your material lined up against the wall, so to speak, and then a door opens quite surprisingly. For me a methodic approach has to be made lively by intuition. Method and intuition are not at all contrary. These are two facets of the same process. Intuition is more or less unconscious; it works by itself, and the method, of course, is something you are very much aware of. Now sometimes method can obscure intuition. So you have to take care to always have the possibility of intuition, but you also must not do away with method, because intuition alone is something like a branch of the total process which includes method.

DI PIETRO: So the Sleepwalker is not so mystical?

BOULEZ: Oh, yes, I mean, you know, on the side of intuition there is a kind of faith in what you are doing and this faith guides you, certainly. But I say each case is a new case. Sometimes you have the idea of the work in front of you, and you say to yourself, "I want this or that to happen." Sometimes you discover the work as you are going along. You might have this approach of the labyrinth, as I call it. Either you construct a big perspective and then you are sure of what you are doing, so that you organize ideas, or you are organizing labyrinths. You may also be discovering, possibly, according to this labyrinth, what you encounter also, say, in the resistance of the material. Then the kind of possibilities you see suddenly—you know, musical possibilities (that you discover at the stage where it is possible to discover something) also have a big impact on you and the work. So, you have always to be very alert and sensitive to what you are doing.

Another way is that sometimes when you are composing a piece, the idea of the piece is constantly there—which is closer to what you are talking about, but which is not quite the same thing as saying the music has always already existed. Therefore for instance, you will find (not only in yourself but in this encounter with other people) that suddenly something will click and it will give you an idea. And after that, maybe a couple of years later, you are surprised by it yourself, but by then you have drawn some conclusions that you will not have had again when you looked at the work after that.

For me, when I compose, the package is very important, not the inside. The inside of the composition as you approach it more and more, when you are listening, will begin to make sense in its details. But for me, the package is important. For instance, the register: If you have a long segment in a register which is very tight and closed, then this place will be a remembrance, not for thematic material or for dynamics, but because it is in the frame. And then the next one will be in another frame—very large, for example. Then you know where you are. I think to compose you have to attach a lot of importance to what I call the envelopes. The envelopes can consist of the register, for instance (that's very important), or the dynamics, or rhythm (quick rhythm or very slow rhythm), and so on. You know, these categories are, for me, the envelope's categories. For the first perception you have of the work, it becomes especially important because it drives you; it shows you the way. From this point of view you can build your own story from the inside, but you know where you are going. Or, you can make a kind of jigsaw puzzle the way I did in some works; pieces like *Symphonies of Winds* by Stravinsky—which, for me, was a very big moment in twentieth-century music—which I used as a model. So, you have structures which come very precisely in the same way which are not varied, particularly, or have very little variation but

are really quite solitary—recognizable, even—because of the register and the way the register is being used. However, you don't know where such structures come in the chronology of the work. If you have A-B, you can have A-C, A again, C-B, and so on. So, you are recognizing these structures, but the moment when they come is absolutely unforeseeable. And then, you have a good perception of the piece, but at the same time your perception is always fooled. And I think, for me, the purpose of a work of art is to make sure that you are perceiving something, but you are never sure of how you perceive it and what you will perceive.

DI PIETRO: Such a composition is so rich, then, that when you come back to the beginning of the work, you can appreciate it so many times in new ways.

BOULEZ: Yes. Because there is always an element of surprise and, at the same time, you are reassured. That's a kind of contradiction or dialectic between sure/not sure.

Originally with the intention of helping Boulez in his search for a writer with whom to collaborate on his new opera, I introduced him to the work of the writer Richard Nelson Peszka, who prepared the first question of this set for Boulez.

DI PIETRO: Your music has always seemed to arise from what Mallarmé described as "the springs of poetry; a unique source." This sense of a world being created anew, almost the birth of sound itself, has been a component of the signature of your authenticity, as well as one of the most compelling aspects of your creative imagination. In the act of composition, have you encountered perennial imaginative structures which, though once

embraced as fertile sources, became obstacles which you then felt prevented you from approaching territories in which you recognized possibilities radically different from those your musical imagination generated innately?

BOULEZ: For me, the question is not in those terms. I think in a kind of irrational evolution, and, by the irrational, I mean something that is not completely rational in my point of view, where I don't want a certain development or unfolding to take place. I am, of course, directing this evolution of my thinking but, at the same time, I am experiencing many influences as I am making discoveries in life. You cannot, for example, read all of the books in the world when you are twenty or twenty-five. You cannot see all the paintings or know a great deal about history, et cetera. So, progressively, you discover something you have never heard of— either something that forms a continuity for you by your own younger generation, or something, even now, by my own generation, at my present age. Let's say you discover a work in the repertoire that you did not know before, and it speaks to you in some way. I discovered, for instance, rather late in life—because in France it was quite unknown there, even as we speak—the poetry of Emily Dickinson. This happened when I was teaching at Harvard in 1963, when my students introduced me to her work. I had no idea of her existence at that time, and I was really taken by the poetry and the letters, especially, which are really extraordinary. In the correspondence of a poet, you find a kind of normal life, you know—statements about the comings and goings of life—but with her, even her daily life is completely transformed. This was so striking for me, that someone could have such an imagination so that even the smallest event becomes something extraordinary. It reminded me of something I already knew much earlier in the diaries of Franz Kafka. By making this parallel be-

tween the correspondence of Dickinson and the diaries of Kafka, continuity was formed in my evolution. In Kafka's diaries, you come upon an incident that occurred when he was on a trip to Paris. He witnessed an accident between an automobile and a tricycle. This was around 1910—I don't remember exactly! This accident becomes a kind of cosmic cataclysm.

Certainly, to describe that fits into that kind of normal life as in the correspondence of Emily Dickinson. However, to see then how Kafka transforms this small, banal incident—this small nothing, really—is quite amazing. I very much admire how those writers are able to make an entire world out of something that was really so small. That, for me, is imagination. People either have imagination or they do not. If you compare Kafka's writings with James Joyce's *Ulysses* (both Kafka and Joyce have been two very strong influences on me), you can see two different ways of handling the imagination. With Kafka, the imagination comes from facts which are quite real and are then progressively twisted until they become completely unreal. With Joyce, you also have quite a real generating object. But the technique he uses to describe an object is completely different from Kafka. In Joyce, an object remains in reality and is not transformed into something unreal. But, I mean, Joyce is also completely extraordinary in his descriptive technique, which leads to the abstract without losing sight of the original object.

DI PIETRO: In a manner related to cubism, perhaps.

BOULEZ: You could say, but to go back to Kafka, that's not his way of description. His German, for instance, is very normal, very easy to read, as opposed to someone like Holderlin, Kafka gives you a very trivial object which is progressively, even very quietly, but completely transformed, so that at the end of one page you don't know where you are anymore. And, for me, that is one of the

functions of art. So, these are the two extremes of imagination, which I like to try to keep together for myself, in my work. Either you transform the object completely, or you describe the object in a different way. This is how I would explain having an influence.

Coming back to your original question: Mallarmé was very influential for me at one point, but now I would not go back to that because it was a period in my life in which I was very involved in the type of influence that I received from Mallarmé. When I look back on that now, I see that time with a distance, of course, because you do not remain where you were in life. I try to find something else so as not to return to the same sources. Sources are for a moment in your life, because an influence happens to coincide with what you want or what you need. The masterpiece speaks about you; you don't speak about the masterpiece—which means that what you look at as a source, from the past or the present even, is nothing more than what you want to find, and coincides with what you were looking for.

DI PIETRO: You speak of development in music as being a more important value for you than mere juxtaposition of ideas in sound. I believe that it is no coincidence that romanticism evolved contemporaneously with what some now call "second-wave industrialization." Might this sense of development that you admire in Beethoven and Wagner be a sort of mirror image—the twin, so to say—of that other mode of development—that is to say, part of that "grid" in Western civilization? Why is it more important for you to develop musical ideas, rather than juxtapose them?

BOULEZ: For me, what is interesting in a work is the trajectory. When talking about musical development, we can define it better by looking at what does not develop in music. For instance, I do not reject what Stockhausen has called "moment form." Stock-

hausen thought he had invented that, but I think moment form
exists already with the lieder of Schumann and Schubert. Songs by
these composers are instant definitions of a type of music which
cannot be expanded, and this also happens in Mahler—for example, when Mahler tries to develop some of the *Songs of a Way-
farer* in his symphonies. It is very strange for me when you have a
kind of quote in these symphonies from *Das Knaben Wunderhorn,* which he cannot develop. You know it's a quote. The idea itself is self-contained, a kind of moment form, and it is impossible
for him to develop this at this point. In a contrary manner, when
you listen to Wagner's *Siegfried Idyll* and then find it in the third
act of *Siegfried* (at the point in the opera where you have the dialogue between Brunhilde and Siegfried), you find the same ideas,
the same thematic motives. In the opera the material is enmeshed
in the fabric of the larger whole of the work itself, not just juxtaposed. But in *Siegfried Idyll* this same thematic material is rather
separated, juxtaposed, and does not really mix well. It is left ex-
posed. With this you have a contradiction, a paradox, which brings
us back to the beginning of your question, because you cannot just
equate development with industrialization. You see in Western
civilization the birth, at a certain moment during the nineteenth
century, of both development and nondevelopment: two types of
formal structures with definite differences between them. You
also see differences between momentlike forms that don't develop, and momentlike forms that might possibly be developed.
From the *Wunderhorn Lieder,* what is quoted within the scherzo
of Mahler's *Symphony No. 3* in one case is developed and in another case is not. You see the possibility of a single idea, which can
be or not be developed according to what the composer wants to
do, and according to the resistance of the ideas themselves. Schumann (a typical example) is obsessed by the symphonies of
Beethoven, but Schumann's ideas were not ready—maybe not

BOULEZ: Yes, that would be a special case. Because, with *Rituel*, you have all the ideas at the very beginning, and, in principle, those ideas never change, although they are varied.

DI PIETRO: Of course, you wrote *Rituel in Memoriam [Bruno] Maderna*, and, after his death, I noticed you conducted *Aura* and a few other works, but since then, I have not seen any performances or recordings of his works by you.

BOULEZ: Well, you know Maderna's was a worse case than mine, as far as the fact that he was constantly conducting and there was not much time for him to compose. Composition was done between two concerts, and when you look at the scores, you see a kind of collage of materials. I don't mean collage of style but a collage of techniques, let's say. In this sense, the works are really fragile, like an object handmade very quickly and under pressure all the time—it seemed to me, at least. Was this by necessity, or did he not feel the need to stay longer and quietly work by himself? I don't know the answer to that. Therefore, the works are really very fragile, unfortunately because he was extremely gifted. These works need editing. Sometimes you even see where he pasted things together, for example. However, now there is a musicologist in Italy who is editing all the Maderna works for the Sacher Foundation. For me that is very necessary; before you get music in order, it has to be cared for.

DI PIETRO: So has this been a stumbling block to your own presentation of his work?

BOULEZ: Yes, because you always find these problems in the parts, for instance, and thus it becomes very difficult to become convinced to perform the work because it's one small thing after

another in rehearsal until it becomes problematic. That's very much a pity, because I would like very much to perform these works. Of course, Maderna knew his métier—that's not the question, not at all—but the works very much need someone to look at them patiently.

DI PIETRO: So for you, imagination in composition, as in the case of Maderna, must be made concrete and clear in the traditional writing of scores even if the techniques are new?

BOULEZ: Yes, of course you can modify and build on notation, but new techniques must not be left unformulated; solutions have to be found so as clear a picture as possible is conveyed to the musician.

HISTORY AND ROOTS

Boulez speaks of how he has changed as he has evolved through musical history. Referring to Jean Genet, Boulez, early in his career wrote, "I like people who are self-taught—that is, those that have done with models that existed before them." This point is of interest in this series of conversations because, in place of a young Boulez welcoming the self-taught as a way of making room for the next generation, now a different Boulez is evident, speaking of the shortcomings of the amateur, as we discuss various musicians in recent history.

DI PIETRO: Years ago Bruno Maderna, in an interview in Chicago toward the end of his career, described Schoenberg's surprise after World War II at seeing his twelve-note method being taken up as a kind of universal language (in theory). Maderna said

that, in reality, the Schoenberg system was only a moment in history, with much in common with another moment in history—namely, the Renaissance. I know that for some time you dedicated yourself to the development of this method as a language, although you have described this process of transformation in your own work as the absorption of influences to the point where they are no longer recognizable. From the point of view of a universal language and "inventing yourself" into something that is true personality, how do you see such composers as Scelsi and Feldman, who seemed to develop more along the lines of the important but marginal outsider, like Varèse. How do they fit in, or do they?

BOULEZ: Well, I will begin with Schoenberg, who is, for me, a more important question than Scelsi and Feldman, who are really marginal for me. I will speak of them later. Yes, certainly I saw that the Schoenberg twelve-tone method was seen (it was propagated first by René Leibowitz, especially) as a kind of universal method of language that was the achievement of many centuries of tradition. Of course, it was obvious, I remember, from the very beginning, that for me it was not the case (proof of this was that I had written rather early that Schoenberg's method was rather restrictive). And, as you know, Schoenberg himself was not completely confident in the system, so he used his method in a very classical framework. He used sonata form, rondo form, and so forth—which proves that his technique was just a way for writing notes or having a kind of relationship with the notes. This was the accomplishment of part of his life. It is true that he tried to pursue the Wagnerian dream: to have everything related to thematic material. The more you go into Wagner, starting with the last part of *The Ring*, the more you see that, practically, there are very few things which are neutral. Many things are related to themes and to thematic material.

With Schoenberg, the further he went, the more his thematic material invaded everything to the point where there is practically no neutral material left.

DI PIETRO: What is "neutral material" in this context?

BOULEZ: I take as neutral material—for instance, material in Bach where you have a fugue—and you can find a kind of rhythm which is neutral. When material is committed to finding all the words in the structure, it becomes a kind of filling material. In Wagner, this filling material that you find in *Rheingold,* you find much less in *Götterdämmerung.* So that's the development of themes and thematic material that Schoenberg pushed to its utmost consequence. Everything in twelve-note writing will depend on a single material. Of course, this method was very restrictive, and Schoenberg felt himself restricted. And you can find that his imagination, although still very powerful, is less powerful than in the pieces where he was composing more freely—as in the writing of *Moses and Aaron,* which is less rich and inventive, in a way, than the invention in *Erwartung.* Certainly there is a loss; there is a gain in construction, in relationships, in structure, and so on, but there is a loss in imagination because you're restricted. And that I felt quite clearly, and, not only that, I felt, if you have to be so strict, then you have to be strict on all levels! And you have to find development which does not depend anymore on the classical structure you have inherited from another vocabulary which does not apply to a new vocabulary. Therefore, that was the discovery of Schoenberg: the intention of relating everything to one single material—a formula, so to speak. So you see this experience was very necessary to go further to find a way of creating material which could be a generator, depending on the organizational level of the work.

You know, in music there are scales and harmonic laws and so on. But you always have laws which are more or less flexible. The same is true in the music of Bach, which is the best example. You have forms which are very constraining, like the fugue canons. If you look at the score of the *Variations for Cembalo* or the *Variations for Organ,* they are really very strict—extremely strict. And Bach could work with this vocabulary. On the other hand, the pieces in the "Preludes" offer a very free use of the same vocabulary. By just following Schoenberg's laws, one would be closed in on one field—a kind of vigorous field—but you would have no possibility of a free domain. And therefore, for me, it was my effort to try to find a relationship between something which is obbligato and something which is free. But, I mean, this experience is essential, and, to tell the truth, individuals like Scelsi or Feldman are amateurs for me. They have fancy ideas and the like, but that's not enough; they have no tools. Varèse had tools. More than that, because he knew how to write, he was not very good at putting a big work together. He is much better in short works because his sense of structure was not very strong. I mean, he had climax after climax; and, to develop ideas, you have to relate them to intention, in moments of rest, and so on. With *Arcana,* for instance, this is a big problem. You have all these areas and successions of climaxes, but the result is segment/segment/segment, with no trajectory. In a short work like *Octandre,* this approach is okay; it works, in fact, because, since the trajectory is so short, the composer can manage. So that was the weakness in Varèse. On the other hand, if you listen to Scelsi—I mean, first, one does not know if he wrote his pieces—that's the main question! I know that he was improvising on a kind of vague electronic instrument and that somebody was transcribing for him. But, I mean, that's very simplistic, certainly; but there are no ideas, just a kind of atmosphere for a couple of bars and extended to nothing. For me, I don't understand really

how it came to be that there has been a kind of big discovery of
Scelsi. Myself, I knew him personally. He was a very intelligent
man—nice and cultivated. But, I mean, he was an amateur, simply
that. I knew him in 1949, so I followed all his developments. You
know, these kind of anarchic people, they are needed from time to
time, because they are subverting the kind of academism to which
everybody finally tends. But, as values, these people's ideas have no
values. I put in this category Satie, Ives, Cage; I put Scelsi and I
put Feldman—people who are provoking thoughts, but who have
not the tools to realize their ideas. Or they realize their ideas in a
much too simplistic way; you can see that in two seconds.

DI PIETRO: As principal guest conductor of the Chicago Symphony, you have inaugurated a Varèse cycle. So Varèse is, for you,
not really marginal, even though he is an outsider?

BOULEZ: Yes, well, I think he is certainly a *kind* of outsider,
and he will remain a kind of outsider. First, because he has composed very few works; and, second, because they are all very
short. So he did not have the time to expand. Really, his big time
was the 1920s and early thirties. After that, he went into a kind
of depression and, practically, did not compose for twenty years.
Or he composed very little. *Déserts,* his last [completed] work
[featuring live performers], was already begun in the thirties. He
finished it because there was a kind of renaissance around him,
so it brought him some energy back to write.

DI PIETRO: Is he still close to your heart?

BOULEZ: Oh, yes, with some reservations. I mean, you know,
in the long run, he does not know really how to organize a composition. He is much better in shorter works, because his mate-

rial is really for that. Like many French people, he does not know how to develop ideas; he just juxtaposes them. And Messiaen is the same, for instance. There is no development in the sense of the Germans, who develop musical ideas: Beethoven, Mahler, and also Wagner, of course. That's also the defect of Liszt, who just juxtaposed things.

And with Varèse, it's a fact. Look at *Amériques*—there is no elaboration of material. All you have are simple juxtapositions, which means that the themes are not different upon their restatement, but are more or less static. Therefore, Varèse is much better in a kind of restricted area; but, in this restricted area, Varèse is very, very strong, you know. Very strong.

DI PIETRO: Could we take another twist on this question of amateurs? For example, Franco Rella, writing on [Georges] Bataille [1897–1962] from the point of view of Italian critical studies of the late seventies, calls Bataille an amateur, but hardly does he say "simply that." If Bataille is a special case regarding this amateur question (and perhaps the historian Phillipe Ariès was another), are there any equivalents in music that fall beyond the category of "simply that"? Would you say, for example, that Xenakis might fall into this special case?

BOULEZ: Yes, I think Xenakis would fall into this category, but I will give you what for me is a better example, and that is the case of Charles Ives versus Gustav Mahler. You know, in both composers there is the interest in popular tunes and quotations, and in Protestant hymns and chorales. But in Mahler you find a completely worked-out and workable integration of this material on a successful level, whereas in Ives, the material rather just hangs together and is never really realized. You have the ideas, of course, but not the solutions, so you do not have a satisfying experience the

way you do with Mahler. So I hold to my previous idea of amateurs, but I do not mean to imply that these people are not without some interest; I am not merely being negative.

DI PIETRO: So when Frances-Marie Uitti wrote me to say that Scelsi "was convinced that, through meditation and improvisation, he could become a channel for higher forces . . . that he considered himself to be a medium to receive inspired music . . . and that he considered the subsequent task of transcribing the music to be for the artisan . . . ."

BOULEZ: I still say no—that is more of an excuse for not writing the music down, similar to the case of Cage, where Cage reached an impasse, and instead of solving the problem, he just accepted the problem as it was. That's the same with Scelsi; these composers do not have the tools, as I said before, to realize their ideas. By contrast, when Mahler was up against an impasse (just as formidable, really), he found the solutions to work out his problems. You know, you cannot begin to compose at forty; it's just not possible. A composer is like an athlete; if you begin at forty, the muscles are just not there anymore. It's the same in the musical realm, if you want to be more than an amateur.

DI PIETRO: John Scoville and I would like to ask a couple of questions concerning your roots. Stravinsky once remarked "that the ordinary musician's trouble in judging composers like Boulez is that he does not see their roots. These composers, like Boulez, have sprung full-grown; the ordinary musician asks 'what sort of music would Boulez write if he was asked to write tonal music?'" Did you indeed spring "full-grown," as Stravinsky seems to have thought, and what has changed since he made these remarks so many years ago?

BOULEZ: First off, I don't think one just comes on the scene full-grown, as Stravinsky thought about me. A composer is like a tree or plant and develops progressively, but that does not mean that others see or know about a composer's development. Secondly, there are some personalities which are defined very early, and there are some which come to bloom much later in life. Each case is different. If you look at, for instance, Messiaen, you see that he was defined very early on. Of course, he had an interesting evolution, but his style and way of writing and conceiving music was practically in place when he was twenty-two. On the contrary, with Carter (and it is interesting to compare Carter with Messiaen, because they are and were the same age), you see that Carter did not begin to be defined until the 1950s, when he was in his forties. This does not mean that Carter was less gifted; it means that his gifts were revealed to him through a kind of very methodical approach, and he discovered himself later in life. For me, this is different than the case of Scelsi, for example. It is the same with Ravel and Debussy. Ravel found himself immediately when he was twenty or twenty-one; and Debussy at that age was very hesitant—he could not define himself very precisely. Yet, it was after Debussy's personality became defined that you see how radical his evolution was, compared with Ravel. Debussy kept going; whereas, with Ravel, you don't see much movement in his evolution—rather, you see him staying in his own territory. Even with Schoenberg, you find something similar, compared to Stravinsky, who wrote the three ballets when he was still young. You have the first period of Schoenberg, which is post-Wagnerian; and then he discovers himself in works like the second quartet through *Pierrot Lunaire*. This was not late in life, because he was not that old, but it was a self-discovery later than Stravinsky's, for instance.

DI PIETRO: So that accounts for Stravinsky's impression, in the 1950s at least, that here was Boulez coming out of nowhere?

BOULEZ: Yes, because he did not know, really, what I had done before—and by that I mean the works I had written in 1946 and '47. When he heard for the first time the *Marteau* [*Le Marteau sans maître*], I was already thirty-two. I was grown up. If he had known the antecedents, Stravinsky would not have been so surprised. But you never just spring full-grown; there is always a process. Even in what we call spontaneous geniuses, like Schubert or Mozart (who are two typical examples), even here, you see an evolution in their output. Although it is true Schubert wrote the *Erlkönig* very early, of course, he also wrote the *Quintet* for strings at eighteen. On the contrary, Mendelssohn wrote his best works when he was very young, and after that his work shows much more métier than genuine inspiration. You cannot generalize this type of thing.

DI PIETRO: Have concert musicians changed since Stravinsky made these remarks?

BOULEZ: Well, Stravinsky means, by "ordinary" musicians, people who don't follow the evolution of certain composers—and, at that time, those composers were Stockhausen and me. We are all born from at least one father or from many fathers. When you are young, you have many influences, and the mixture of all these influences makes your personality. You take from these fathers exactly what you want and need. It is a kind of food that you feel is necessary for your intellectual life. It can also happen that, later in life, you discover things you did not know when you were young, and you benefit from these late discoveries, too. For instance in my case, I knew Wagner early on, but not Mahler. Then I learned the Viennese school of Schoenberg, Berg, and Webern in between; so I discovered Mahler later in life, because Mahler was not performed in France when I was young. In this way, I discovered the

missing link in this tradition. Even so, I had a notion of the continuity within the Germanic tradition even though at that time I did
not see the real continuity.

SCOVILLE: If I am hearing you correctly, I have a sense that
there is not a single definition to Pierre Boulez. In many ways, what
Rocco hopes for is to go beyond a single definition. What I gather,
from what you said, is that you are an organic being continually processing over time these various fathers, if you will, into absorption.

BOULEZ: Yes, I'm interested in the organic, because it is something that completely alters the direction—one might say the
"forecast"—of the work. The forecast is similar to what we were
talking about in another conversation in reference to Cage. A composer is going in a certain direction but at the same time takes into
account the accident, which is the unforeseen. I don't like these
theocratic visions that we find in say, Schoenberg, or the all-
encompassing formula you find in Stockhausen. Such approaches
are antinomic to my way of thinking. I need, or work, with a lot of
accidents, but within a structure that has an overall trajectory—
and that, for me, is the definition of what is organic.

SCOVILLE: I was fascinated with the idea that you were conducting Mahler. Mahler has so much of a metaphysical quality
about him; yet you, I feel, are very French. From my point of
view, the French tradition is much more objective. This is even
true with the surrealists, who step away and are not so metaphysical in their sensibilities. So it is a mystery for me to see
Pierre Boulez between these two ideas. How do you relate to
these two different traditions (the subjective and the objective),
which, in a sense, have two different values? You don't see yourself like Heinrich Heine, do you?

BOULEZ: No, it is different for me. I think I was always attracted to the German tradition, because the French tradition, when I was young, was completely degraded. That is, it was no longer any more Debussy and Ravel, but Poulenc and Auric and so on—a tradition that is not at all on the same level as the pervious one. Therefore, the French tradition was something I put aside. The French had, of course, Stravinsky (who was a disturbance in the national culture who was then adopted by France) and, to a degree, Bartok as well. But Stravinsky was the center of music in France. Therefore, I wanted to discover the German tradition which, for me, was very important. When I went to live in Germany around 1958, I was completely involved in that culture, bringing, of course some of my traditional French education with me. I tried (not consciously, of course) to make a mixture of these two cultures. The good side of French musical culture is sound, which is important for me. Good French composers are always very sensitive to the sound aspect of composition. It does not mean that German composers don't care about the sound aspect. Wagner is always very careful about the sound aspect. But somewhere in the French tradition (actually, there is no tradition in France)—with composers like Berlioz, Debussy, and Ravel—the material of the sound is as important, or even more important, than the content. For example, in Berlioz sometimes the musical content is very thin, but the sound is absolutely marvelous. Also in Liszt, the content is sometimes rather shallow, but, say, in his piano writing, it is fantastically interesting (in composers you have different levels of interest). The harmonic language of Berlioz is very gauche and tortured. The harmonic language of Chopin is, on the contrary, extremely interesting. So there are few composers who can have this balance between content, form, style, and sound. Wagner is one of the rare examples of balance—like Debussy later, although on a smaller scale, and so is Mahler. Es-

pecially late Mahler is an example of the right balance between all
of these qualities. I think I now understand the Austro-Germanic
culture much more than I did thirty or forty years ago.

CAGE AND CHANCE

John Cage's indeterminacy is not Pierre Boulez's *aléa*. Boulez discussed his concepts of chance and how he differs from Cage on this
most seminal topic of the twentieth century.

DI PIETRO: In 1989, Francis Bacon made a remark in an interview [with Michael Peppiatt], "Provoking Accidents and Prompt-
ing Chance," that chance and accident are the most fertile elements at any artist's disposal at the present time. Yet, he never took
this as far as, say, Jackson Pollock, and he did not really believe in
the automatism of Andre Masson or the surrealists. Is there a parallel here with your own work vis-à-vis your early correspondence
with John Cage and your later ideas as expressed in *Aléa*?

BOULEZ: Yes, what Bacon and I did with chance is very different from what Cage did with chance. For example, in my work,
what I call accidents, or things that just happen, are accepted into
the work as a whole. That's very different from pure chance, like
Cage, where you set the work up so that practically nothing will
happen but accidents. Pure chance, in this sense, brings you anything that happens and, in fact, not very much does happen, or
something happens once in ten thousand times. Statistically, that's
not very interesting. With Cage, you open the window and listen
to the noise on the street, as if it was a piece of music practically. I
don't think things are as simple as that, and, therefore, the kind of

chance operation that Cage did was never of great interest to me. There is no directionality in this kind of thinking, no involvement in just accepting what is there or what has come up. So, that was where we split, intellectually. And even if you are just selecting things that you want to happen within this rigid framework for the purpose of getting rid of your emotions, that's not of great interest.

What Francis Bacon and I agree on in the use of chance is that you should not be rigid with a theory about what you are doing. Making a program out of, say, the tossing of coins, as a technique and not deviating from what the program says or what you have decided the meaning is—that's a theocratic kind of vision, and I think it is against all kinds of artistic creativity.

So, for me, accepting what happens in a work is very different from Cage's indeterminism. Let me give you an example. Say I have decided to create a new piece, and the material I am working with does not accept what I have decided is its current meaning. At that point, the material will put me on another path, so I might find another way. I have to accept this kind of thing. If, for instance, while I am composing this piece I happen to be reading another score or looking at a painting and, suddenly, it gives me an idea, I can include this in the material I am working with in the piece. That is what I (and, certainly, Bacon) mean by accepting what happens. It means that you can deviate intelligently, as he did, with consequence, and not just accept what has happened, like suddenly coming on a scratch in the paper. That is not terribly interesting. So, if you have something you have seen or heard which is interesting, even if it did not belong to your thinking at the beginning, then you have to integrate what has happened to your current thinking in this moment.

DI PIETRO: Last time, we were speaking of certain composers you called anarchists. You said there were no values in their ideas.

I am interested in this idea that within much of modernism there could be values. Can values be equated with content? Comparing your work with, for example, Morton Feldman's, do you consider your own to have content (from the point of view that much of the twentieth century after World War I has been about the loss of values)? So, what are values if . . . .

BOULEZ (bursting in): It depends on what you call "values"! For me, the first value in music is to know what to do and how to do it. Although Cage was a very nice and a very inventive man, in a way, he had no tools; that is the main thing. It you are a composer, or a painter, or a writer, the main thing is to have the tools to do your work. It does no good to just write the letters of the alphabet, one after the other, without any consequence, without any logic. You, at least, have to have the logic of the words, if only that. Then you must have the logic of grammar, as well as the logic of constructions, phrasing, and so on. These kinds of tools, which everyone accepts in life, can, of course, be used in many ways. There are many ways of using a language and not just a unique way, but the basics of the language should be there. What disturbs me, then, is when the basic grammar is not there, when the technique and the vocabulary are not there. Invention without tools is really not very much because everybody has ideas, *everybody*, especially when you are young—you have a lot of inventiveness in yourself. But the main thing is to organize that inventiveness and to make it really fruitful, rather than just accept whatever happens.

In the past, when you look at all the sketches Beethoven did to find a theme, for instance—that's really extraordinary. I am conducting Mahler's *Fourth Symphony* this evening. When I look closely at the score to see how things are organized, this organization should not be prominent. It should be a tool, precisely, and not the goal of the work. This is very important to me, that the

technical aspect, or what I could call the "tool," generally, is simply a way of doing things—of organizing things, in bringing new ideas to light and in generating other ideas. All of that is a kind of genetics, because ideas do generate other ideas. If you do not know how to do this, if you just have, let's say, *flashes*, where you don't reach out and connect all of this material, that is what I mean by not having tools or values, which I would describe as "knowing what to do and how to do it." This is why the technical side of things is so absolutely essential.

DI PIETRO: One of Jean-Paul Sartre's central issues was one of responsibility and authenticity. From what I know of you, it is very important for you to be authentic in what you compose. In other words, you are taking responsibility for that composition in the sense of the tools which you have been discussing, so that what you want to express is derived from a model and is very carefully couched in terms of expression. You then try to evoke something in terms of collective hysteria, in order to provoke in the audience a genuine response.

BOULEZ: Yes, that is true, but I make a distinction between responsibility and authenticity because everyone is authentic. You know, people think they express themselves authentically, yet authenticity can be foolishness because you think you are true, but, as a matter of fact, you don't bother to have the tools to be true. So the word *authentic* should be taken very carefully because it can be a smokescreen: "Ah! Authenticity! Ah! Being open with oneself!" and so on. That's very nice, but that is not the problem. The problem, for me, is responsibility. Yes.

SCOVILLE: For me, at least, it seems that Cage would craft a piece in a responsible way, in that the musicians must do certain

things. After that, however, there is no responsibility because the expressive quality for the piece is no longer at hand. It seems to me that you take a jump in which you do take responsibility for your pieces, in the sense that you are trying to evoke a specific or, at least, a general response in the audience. Cage denies this. He says that he has done this thing and that whatever happens is okay.

DI PIETRO: I have just read the Cage interviews with Joan Retallack. I very much regret that Cage is no longer with us to ask what he would now think of this concern we have touched on concerning responsibility.

BOULEZ: If you look at what Cage did when he took two or three radios (and I've seen this piece performed), where he puts, say, 98.3 on the dial and then, after five seconds or so, he changes the setting to 100.3 and waits fifteen seconds. Well, that's not taking responsibility—that is making a diagram without content really, and in that I find a total lack of responsibility. It can be amusing, it can be surprising, but it does not happen twice. For me, that is one of the main criteria: to be able to produce an event more than once. Now, even if the event is surprising and you may or may not be pleased, the second time you go through a kind of apprenticeship in which you get to know the work, really. Then, once you know the work, even when you go through the repetition of events, the work still remains a mystery. For me that is very important. But with the radio piece of Cage's, you have no mystery or a very small sense of mystery at the beginning when you wonder what will happen next, but after that, the mystery is gone. This is the main problem that I see. If the work does not sustain a critical analysis and if the mystery does not subsist and does not remain after that, then the work is worth nothing. That is my opinion, and it does not apply only to Cage. It can apply to

anything which is written very quickly or is overly pleasant—which is going on right now, or even the overly simple and so on. The authentic, for me, then, is the typical smokescreen for people who have nothing to say or who have very trivial things to say.

SCOVILLE: By the "overly pleasant," you mean this trend for saccharine, pleasant music in the concert world in general?

BOULEZ: Yes.

SCOVILLE: And this pleasant music has very little to do with current reality, if you take the trouble to look around the world, let alone take responsibility for anything.

DI PIETRO: This goes back to what we were discussing the last time when you [Boulez] talked about people taking refuge from current reality which has no room for feelings. But what about the "overly simple"?

BOULEZ: We spoke of this previously when we spoke of the neoromantic. But you know there are many ways of approaching the problems of music today. However, when you have composers like Wagner or Mahler behind you, to take two examples (and for me, I was challenged by their solutions), you cannot then say that they did not exist or that they were too complex so now I am going to do something simple. The human being is really complex—the human being is not simple—and I find these kinds of simplistic solutions contradictory to humanity, as when, for example, the Stalinists in the late 1940s went around saying "people should be happy." Sometimes these solutions do remind me of fast-food restaurants, which can be convenient but are completely without interest.

DI PIETRO: I have heard you say this somewhere before, but this also goes back to what we were talking about when you said, "Composers exist in relation to many factors not determined by themselves," that "we all think we are individuals who have created our own world," as some might say in response to your idea of the overly simple. It could be said that your response is too overly historical, or even overly socialized—why not try to wipe out the past with something simple if it corresponds to a need? But you are saying that this notion is an illusion of sorts, and absolutely impossible to achieve, because we are, in reality, all extremely connected?

BOULEZ: In reality we are all extremely dependent.

DI PIETRO: Many people have been reading, with great interest, the long-awaited English translation of the Boulez–Cage correspondence of the 1950s. Your letters to Cage taper off into silence as the volume progresses. . . .

BOULEZ: The problem of Cage, at this time of the correspondence, began for me in the development of the prepared piano, which at a certain point I was no longer able to follow. John Cage's prepared piano was an instrument capable of producing, by means of an artificial tablature, complexes of frequencies. It is an artisanal tablature in which one places between the string such different materials as metal, wood, rubber: materials that modify the characteristics of the sound produced by the vibrating string. As you know, I was fascinated by Cage's prepared piano and wrote about it early on—welcoming it, as it seemed to offer an artificial, embryonic, but plausible solution to avoiding the clichés of the old tonal language. The problem with the prepared piano for me was that, as a sound-producing mechanism, it let in all kinds of noises that would never be transferable in a hierarchy of sound.

For example, an everyday noise that may come out of a prepared piano—a knock of wood on a metal table—always sounds like a table being rapped, no matter what the context. This is only one of many examples of this sort I could cite. Cage, faced with this impasse, decided to just accept these noises, and by extension whatever else happened as part of the composition. Of course, he explained all this by way of Zen and mysticism or whatever, in a kind of psychological reverse, but this for me was just an excuse for not facing up to this paradox, and when I saw this, of course, I was disappointed in something I thought had shown great promise. This was just the beginning, as I saw the direction in which he was going. Instead of stepping back and analyzing this prepared-piano problem (which was basically one of heterophony) and solving this impasse, he just accepted the situation as it was, and later this acceptance of whatever happens got into his composing on other levels, as everybody knows. So, of course, as I saw this, the letters became less and less. I was no longer interested in his development, but he was a friend whom I liked nonetheless.

STOCKHAUSEN AND ZAPPA

DI PIETRO: Have you had any contact with Stockhausen lately? What do you think of his series of operas?

BOULEZ: Well, it is very difficult for me to speak about that because I have never seen them. They have not been performed in France. There was one occasion when we commissioned a part of one of his operas, but it was not on stage and was a concert version with our ensemble, back in 1977. So that's long ago, when he wrote for us *Michael's Journey*. I think there is a very

big difference between the music of Stockhausen's operas and the stage or theatrical conception.

DI PIETRO: On the surface, at least, it seems that you might have a lot of parallels. We talked about opera last time.

BOULEZ: Yes, for me, on the good side of it, Stockhausen does not accept the conventions of the opera house; that for me is a big thing, very positive. But the literary aspect is for me really very difficult to accept. Because he's preoccupied with Wagner's concept of the "total" work, which puts all his projects in Wagner's shadow, let's say. But at least in the dramas of Wagner you have at least literature, maybe not the best literature within German literature, but it is a very strong dramatic invention. Ah, with Stockhausen, I don't find that. I find the musical aspect better than the dramatic aspect.

DI PIETRO: So there are points of contact you might have with the music of Stockhausen?

BOULEZ: Yes, but I find sometimes that the thematic material is not very interesting—what he actually does with it, I mean, is not very rich. And then what he calls the formula is maybe too much deterministic; it's already there before you have written anything. For example, you build the cupboard first and then you put the content inside. For me it's the opposite: you create the content and you make the cupboard because of the content and not on the contrary; so that's a different approach. The more I thought about it, the less I was ready to conceive of a form (just like that—all by itself). For me, I discover the form progressively as I go on. So again, it's an organic process. You could, for instance, have proportions of time. Some are this long; some are

that long within the structure. Then you have to fill up the proportions of time with material that may not be up to that duration of the formula, calling for some kind of development. If you
observe these proportions as part of the formula very strictly,
sometimes the material will not be very rich. For me, sometimes
you have the material in the cupboard which is so rich, that its
development calls for more expansion; or, on the contrary, the
material may not support a long development so you have to reduce the proportions of the structure—that is, the cupboard.
But your decision is made not before, but afterward, when you
are working with the material during its actual composition.

DI PIETRO: So that your actual process of composition is your
actual process of life?

BOULEZ: Yes, like an organism, in which the cells develop in an
organic way.

DI PIETRO: So it does not matter what soil you are in; it will grow.

BOULEZ: Yes, the soil is the musical idea, which allows for organic growth. If you try to insert yourself into history on purpose,
like the Stravinsky of the neoclassical period, you see that that does
not come off. The real historical Stravinsky was when he was creating *The Rite of Spring*. That is real history, even though it was a
break with history. When he was composing *Oedipus Rex*, he was
not in history at all—in my opinion, at least. You cannot be the hen
and the egg at the same time. That's impossible!

DI PIETRO: You mentioned the formula in Stockhausen, but
recently in an interview with Andrew Ford, he denies this. He

claims the most urgent question of the second half of the twentieth century is the problem of combining intuition and preplanning. He admits that recently he has broke open his own
construction (the formula) and felt terribly ashamed, like someone who has sinned terrifically. "Sins against his own rules," he
called it. But for him these "sins" (or the answer to the formula
problem) seem to be "sound visions" within pluralism, like the
recent helicopter string quartet which came to him in a dream.
There are two questions here: (1) Is the most urgent compositional question the combination of intuition with preplanning,
and (2) Is there any alternative to pluralism?

BOULEZ: I have seen the score to this helicopter string quartet,
and I think that intuition and the frame of the work are one of the
most important compositional questions—that's right. I found that
Stockhausen was completely taken by this formula idea, and finally
at one point it seemed to me it was like a cupboard, which you have
to fill up with things. There is nothing organic about it; there is no
form. It is from my point of view something preconceived. I would
say more than just intuition, organic development is a consequence
of intuition, which is a combination of intuition and order. This
kind of dialectic between a real form and a preconceived idea,
when you are developing your musical ideas with the material,
brings us back to what I called before "accepting the accident." You
make room for this accident within the development of the work
like a mutation—that I call organic. This modification is a mutation
of your ideas which changes the cupboard, like a plant that a gardener has moved from one part of the garden so that its relationship to the light has changed. Well, the plant will go to the sun.
That's what I mean by an accident within organic development. It
needs intuition, but at the same time my musical needs are to draw
from musical ideas' consequences. To go back to your question of

the sleepwalker, I cannot say like Schoenberg that the whole work is in my head like a vision and then all that is left is to just write it down. I don't believe that. Again, this theocratic vision: God created the light—here is the light; God created water and air—here is water and air. This is a God-like view of creativity which I don't believe at all, since I myself believe very much in accidents.

DI PIETRO: Yes. Is that also then within this idea of pluralism? Are your accidents part of an alternative to pluralism?

BOULEZ: It depends what you call pluralism. Is it pluralism of style? Pluralism of what?

DI PIETRO: Stockhausen calls them sound visions.

BOULEZ: What is a sound vision?

DI PIETRO: He says it is something beyond the collage . . . .

BOULEZ: For me a sound vision is something for itself. Sound can be like that. I remember very vividly when I transformed this piece *Sur Incises* that the sound was not there immediately. In the beginning, I thought that I wanted to impose a woodwind sound with the piano, but that would have been a completely different organism, and the ideas would have gone in another direction. What I wanted here was the idea of a mirror of the piano sound modified by the percussion and harp, also the idea of echoes mirroring the same type of sonority. With the woodwind idea, that would have been totally different if not completely impossible. The sound for me cannot really be preconceived, because it is an integral part of the musical conception. Yet sometimes you do have the sound before.

Let me give you some examples. When I composed *Eclat,* I remember I wanted to make sound only with resonating instruments and with a variety of instruments whose resonance was varied—for instance, from the mandolin, which has a very short resonance, to the piano in the low register, which has a much longer resonance. So I had the sound idea before the work was written. On the contrary, with *Sur Incises* the resonance is practically the same between the pianos, harps, and percussion. This allowed me at the end of the work to make sections in the score where I no longer beat the tempo, and the piano listens to its own resonance performing with suspended rhythm. That is exactly the contrary of what I did in *Eclat.* In *Répons* this sound resonance, especially with the electronic transformation, makes the piano resonance much longer, and I had to deal with that. All these sound resonances of the electronics affect the instruments, which are transformed. I had to think of making these resonances in phase with what one hears with the six solo instruments.

DI PIETRO: Yes, so it's very, very different from Stockhausen! Stockhausen, in fact, considers himself a spiritual or even religious composer, and I think that is where this formula comes from.

BOULEZ: Yes.

DI PIETRO: Whereas you have indicated that the esoteric is very nice, but it is too simple.

BOULEZ: Yes.

DI PIETRO: You said that there is more to heaven and earth than the esoteric, and one would never, in any case, be as complex as nature.

SCOVILLE: That reminds me of Michelangelo, when Stock-hausen said that when he makes this transformation of breaking his own rules and feels like a sinner, you saw that in the Renaissance.

BOULEZ: Yes, but you know, I find that this *is* the way of think-ing of Stockhausen, and if he feels that way, then he is right! It is not for me to say otherwise—although this idea of making a big splash with the helicopter string quartet makes me think of Hamlet when he said, "Even if I would be in a nutshell I would be the king of space." I find that that is more important [general laughter]—to be in a nutshell, rather than to fly into space. That's my view of things.

DI PIETRO: You brought Frank Zappa's work to Ircam [Interna-tional research center for computers and acoustic music] and con-ducted some of his works yourself. Could you tell me about this, and how you view the interaction between his work and yours? Are you aware that since then there have been other cross-fertiliza-tions? For example, John Zorn paid an homage to you by rework-ing material from your *Le Marteau sans maître* in a work of his loosely based on Genet and calling it *Elegy*.

BOULEZ: No, I did not know that about Zorn. You know, I don't want to be snobbish or snooty simply because I don't belong to the pop world! I think that would be completely stupid and short-sighted. I like the vitality of these people. I like very much that some of them who are the most gifted make these efforts to have a vo-cabulary, which is more interesting and sophisticated than the vo-cabulary that they use generally. Zappa was very much aware of that. The models that he had, especially Varèse, show you that he was in-terested in going further. So Zappa knew he needed a more sophis-ticated language and that would make him very different than oth-ers in his generation; finally he could not stay with his old language.

DI PIETRO: I just performed in a piece by Zorn, and I think something very similar might be said about him.

BOULEZ: The real problem for me is to mix this vitality with real knowledge. Because if you have too much knowledge, you lose the vitality very often, and you become academic. This is completely the case with serial music, which has produced many examples of academicism, which has become completely sterile. These people know how to write, but without any life. For me there is very little point in that. I prefer people who have vitality and who have the possibility of going above themselves; that, at least, is potential— people who are transgressing their limits. I like people who are transgressing their limits, in any case, and who have the desire to transgress. Therefore, I was very interested in knowing Zappa, which was a world completely different than mine. I felt it was a great benefit to be involved in this work with Zappa. You know, I wanted to invite him back, but it was near the end and he was very sick, and everything collapsed.

2

LISTENING AND THE "OTHER"

In a preconcert talk in Chicago before a fascinating program of *Le Visage nuptial* and *The Miraculous Mandarin,* Boulez spoke to the audience on how to approach this music. I was impressed with the advice he gave them. Rather than attempting to analyze the work to understand its meaning, he suggested that they try to "find themselves in the work." Suddenly one recognizes a part of oneself. There, in front of you, this illuminating part of the work seems "to take possession of you and increase your human potential, your grasp, your power."

Boulez gave, as an example, the story of the mandarin who refuses to die, no matter what blows life has in store for him. As long as he still has desire (for life), and then only when his desire for the girl is satisfied, his wounds begin to bleed and he dies. Boulez told the audience that he found this very moving and, in fact, that there was something profound there, a part of the human experience.

DI PIETRO: Backstage after the concert, I told you that, for me, the combined *Visage* and *Mandarin* resonated together in a realm

very similar to Bataille's work *Eroticism: Death and Sensuality*. As a composer, I was very open to this approach of finding a part of yourself in the work. How successful do you think you have been in getting the audience to listen in this way to relatively unfamiliar works? Could it contribute to building new audiences for the symphony orchestra? Could you elaborate on that? It seems people do that with novels all the time.

BOULEZ: Yes, generally people are listening with other patterns in their minds. For instance, they know a certain literature. They are accustomed to this literature, and they are accustomed to both the literature and to the vocabulary: some chords, some connections of chords with one another, et cetera, and so on and so forth. So, they seek according to these patterns, generally, some patterns that are preformed in their minds. And the same with the structure. They are accustomed to a certain thematic structure which they can follow. So when they hear a work, generally, they come more or less with this prepared mind, even unconsciously. And then they try to find a way of grasping a work with a method which does not require that at all.

We did an experiment at Ircam which was very interesting. A man who was a perception psychologist did some experiments. A Mozart or Haydn sonata was played and, after that, one of the "Klavierstücke" of Stockhausen. And the research team did this with different types of people—you know, some not musicians at all, some not cultivated at all, and some who were professional musicians.

DI PIETRO: Interesting.

BOULEZ: The researchers asked the subjects to describe the form of the music, what they heard. And, of course, the people without any education were confused, in any case, in Mozart or

Stockhausen, because they could not recognize themes. And the more you approached the work with musicians, of course, Mozart or Haydn had no secrets; these listeners could describe the structure quite well—amateur musicians in amateur terms, and professional musicians in professional terms. But when it came to Stockhausen, where the pattern can be taken differently—for instance, when you have a strong accent which is made in the middle of the structure, which can be taken as the beginning of the structure—the analyses were absolutely different by either professional or nonprofessional. It was completely different because everybody tried to put different categories in it. Here the musicians were listening with the intention of finding something, and they were describing their own fantasies. And it was very interesting from this point of view, but, I mean, at the same time, it proves that when you are listening to a work you are making your own movie, let's say. And that I find interesting because nobody hears, I suppose, in the same way. It reminds me of an anecdote. When, for instance, there is an accident on the street, and you have people who were there, not a single one, practically, will give the same account of the facts they have looked at. Because they look at the accident in a different way: one person sees this car; the other sees another car more than the other. Everybody has a personal point of view, and it shows in their perception of the experience.

And in music or in the perception of a work of art, that's exactly the same. I suppose everybody has a different approach because the mind works differently. Certainly, also for me, the richness of the music, strong music, is that everybody should be convinced that he has the right solution for himself. Because it is the purpose of art, finally. You know, somebody who hears the *Missa Solemnis* of Beethoven will follow the words in the "Gloria," but if you ask them afterward what they remember (apart from maybe the last fugue and "Amen"), they will remember a kind of jumble of things.

They will remember, "Yes, that was dramatic" or "This was less dramatic." The listener will construct his own theater from this material. In Schoenberg's *Erwartung,* what the listener follows is the plot, which is rather dark. The main point will be when the woman discovers the corpse—or seems to discover the corpse. Then you have a big climax, and after that, you have quite a lot of different things going on. Certainly, some things will remain very precise, and some things will be quite confused.

DI PIETRO: Could you talk about the programming of the *Visage nuptial* with *The Miraculous Mandarin*? As I said before, it was a juxtaposition that I found interesting.

BOULEZ: Well, when I make a program like that, it is not so much the content of the work, although there may be some of that, but rather the context in which they are put together. For instance in the Bartok, it is a continuous work, from beginning to end. With the *Visage,* it is a work in five parts which is quite different, and forms a juxtaposition, structurally. So it was on purpose that these works were opposed, as form, as content, as vocabulary. I could have put a Schoenberg work—say, the *Variations*—but I did not want to touch that particular work in this context, favoring instead the Bartok with the *Visage.* So you see a little how my approach to programming goes. I like to build programs in a way that there is something coherent and on all of the levels of form: content, vocabulary and structure, and not just in similarities but often in contrasts. Tonight, for instance, I have the Ravel *Tombeau de Couperin,* which is extremely neoclassical contrasted with the Debussy *Two Images,* which are very impressionistic. The same language—with just a touch of Spanish in the Debussy, which gives the cue for *The Spanish Hour* by Ravel, which follows on the second half of the program.

What is the "other"? For a long time with respect to Western civilization, it was "non-Western" cultures. After an astounding performance of the restored version of Edgar Varèse's *Ameriques* with 150 musicians in Orchestra Hall (Chicago), I went backstage and remarked to Boulez that "Native Americans did not have a chance." The composer-conductor took one of his famous about-faces. I quickly gathered my thoughts and said, "No, no, I mean in the sense that this work could be seen to represent a terrifying multiheaded monster of certainty that is Western civilization itself; with that kind of naïveté one literally becomes a god." The maestro turned around and gave me a penetrating look, to which I said, "Could we discuss the 'other'?"

DI PIETRO: What I find of interest is some of the changed views you now hold, compared with the past. At one point you even mentioned your evident delight in these "contradictions," as you put it, quoting Baudelaire. For example, your interest in being in touch with people and cultures who have other concepts—you now perceive the misunderstandings that arise as fruitful, because what you see in another culture is what you want that other culture to reveal about yourself. But I am thinking also of an earlier article you wrote on the interaction between Eastern and Western music, questioning the fruitfulness of such confrontations. In light of some of the ideas which you now hold, it seems that the answer proposed in the past to that interaction is now something very different. Is that true?

BOULEZ: You could say I was very influenced when I was young by cultures of Asia and Africa. But I saw these cultures from a very different point of view than that of the original cultures. I could not pretend that I understood them. I understood them not from their point of view; I understood them from my point of view,

which is completely different. And that I called a misunderstanding—a misunderstanding because, fundamentally, what you pick up is the kind of impression you have of the music you hear. For instance, I remember very well the first time I heard the court music in Japan, or Chinese theater music, or the music of Bali. Of course, it was a revelation! That world of sound that I did not know at all. What was its religious meaning? What was the meaning of the music with respect to the dance? What was the mythology that was the basis to it all? Just listening in the beginning, I heard the periodicity. I asked, "Why this instrument?" "Why these instruments?" And so on. So, possibly, I began to understand more but I cannot say that I still understand, really, the music of Bali from the *Balinese* point of view. I think, for me, I will certainly analyze it, more or less—even if I try to do so in a different way. I will analyze it from the point of view of a man in the Western world—in terms of periodicity, in terms of regularity, in terms even of some continuity of sixteenth notes, for example, in the rhythm. However, when the people of Bali play this music, they don't think like that at all. So, when I am listening, I am putting my own grid of analysis on it. Therefore, I say that it is a misunderstanding because I take what I think is before me. With this kind of relationship, I want to open my mind, because I am very fascinated by this culture; but, given my education, what I want to get from this culture is something more than a kind of purely superficial relationship. You know, I can imitate the music of Bali, of course. With a vibraphone and so on, and with regularity of pulse and using pentatonic scales, imitation could be very easy; but if you want to go beyond that, then you have to put your own grid of values on this music and demonstrate, for instance, what it means to you. For me, Balinese music is a kind of immobility, harmonic immobility. You have to think in more general terms. Another example: If I hear the gagaku Japanese court music (as I well remember hear-

ing it in 1945 or '46), the first thing which is very impressive is the expansion of time, because the sustained pace of this music is very slow for a long time. And that's completely different from our conceptions of time. A related phenomenon is the use of small intervals in gagaku—intervals which do not seem to move. This is a kind of destruction of the intervals. And that, for me, was very important because I speak in my own terms when I speak of the category of time. That's comparing my perception of gagaku time with what we are doing here, generally, in Western civilization— namely, to go from a point to another point, which is moving and developing. On the contrary, here in gagaku, I had the impression that the music is completely static. I could give you many examples of this, a kind of "creating," which is very important. And I think, in a way, that every contact means you are always in the process of misunderstanding something, because you need something, and at one point you see it anywhere. Therefore, I find the misunderstanding which is creative to be much more interesting for me than the right understanding, which is not creative.

DI PIETRO: So there's renewal in that.

BOULEZ: Yes. And often you don't hear your misunderstandings in the same ways later, for instance, if you return to a score ten years later. You can take other lessons from the same music after a period of time has passed, because you are looking for something else. And sometimes when you go back to a work which was very strong for you, you say, "Did I really seek that from that piece?" because, you know, you cannot see it in the same way.

DI PIETRO: There is something profound about *Rituel*, its depth. It reminds me of Holderlin, with its presence/absence formula into uncertainty, when Holderlin writes, "And suffering

humanity falls downwards through the ages." Have you ever considered, psychologically speaking, that your life has come out of a trance experience?

BOULEZ: It is a strange work, but I would have liked for you to have heard it the way I played it recently at the Cité de la musique, with the groups far apart. The audience was in the middle, and I was conducting in the middle of the audience, but we were separated from each other spatially. This made for a very independent and very clear sonority acoustically. Also, I had programmed for the first part of the concert traditional Japanese gagaku music. Gagaku was always very interesting to me, and the audience was struck by the fact of the similar concepts of time—these long sounds—with a different vocabulary. So for me it was a striking experience that I want to renew, this parallel between the Japanese ritual with its concept of time and the *Rituel* of mine. So in the next performance of *Sur Incises* I will program the music of Bali before it is performed. It will be with authentic instruments, of course, with its typical continuity of the pulse. Then *Sur Incises* will follow. Again, not in the style of Balinese music, but one will hear parallels with the continuous nature of the pulse. I like to compare not only my work but other work generally with the work of another culture, to see how a confrontation can be established between these two worlds.

DI PIETRO: Yes, so it is not so much a personal, psychological thing, that this was a trance experience for you, speaking of *Rituel*?

BOULEZ: Yes, that's right. It was really a ceremony, and the idea of a ceremony. Berio had asked me for a piece to mark the occasion of Maderna's death, and I remembered that he was a excellent and very able conductor especially of all kinds of groups within the

orchestra. This ceremony was to have each group congregate more and more and become diverted and diffuse until practically there is a kind of confusion. Yet in *Rituel* you have always the pulse which is more and more imposing as you go on, where everyone is reassembled after straying away. Also, you have a very strange change of perception. At the beginning of the work you don't hear very much percussion. You hear very clearly the oboe and two clarinets, but the more the groups come in, the less you pay attention to the pitch and the more you pay attention to the rhythm. So there is a kind of reverse in the ceremony when the big chords like clouds happen; you don't listen anymore to sentences, but you hear the rumor of the clouds—and that I want to reproduce, a kind of general feeling where the individual is no more important, a measurement in time, which is different in each group and becomes continuous. After all, not a single percussionist can follow the other percussionists. So you have to pay attention to this; it is so irregular, and yet the beat is very even, but even in different ways. So you have the general impression of multiple dimensions of time.

DI PIETRO: A piece about relativity and yet, with the passing of the individual, a kind of presence/absence, as you noted in the dedication, now put beside the culture of Bali in an homage to the other.

BOULEZ: Yes.

ARTISTS, WRITERS, AND OPERA

The intellectual tradition is different than the scholarly tradition. Scholars are interested in information, whereas intellectuals tend to

be artists, musicians, and writers who look at an organic kind of concept of the world around them. In speaking of Jean Genet and Samuel Beckett and the dramatic influences on Boulez, Peter F. Stacy, in his book *Boulez and the Modern Concept,* writes:

> Genet threatens our conception of reality and forces us into different levels of perception: this is where his significance for Boulez probably resides. [With Beckett a] comparison can be made with Boulez's *Structures,* where Boulez claimed that he aimed for an effect of absurdity and disorder.

I wondered if any such parallels could be made with the painter Francis Bacon.

As part of Boulez's seventieth birthday celebration in Chicago, an interesting exhibit was presented in Orchestra Hall of Boulez's manuscripts and items from his personal collection. I don't know why it surprised me to seen in his collection three small paintings by Francis Bacon, dedicated to "Pierre."

DI PIETRO: There is a question that goes along with this surprise of mine. For example, it is very difficult for many people to understand the phenomenon of people like Bacon or Jean Genet. People who in their private lives have been very near disenfranchisement (to say the least) are then later taken up by large institutions, almost as consciences of the nation. It would be very difficult to imagine a U.S. government-sponsored center dedicated to the work of William S. Burroughs. How has it come about that such anarchists as Bacon or Genet have been seen by institutions that represent their cultures as being people of value? Are there any musical equivalents?

BOULEZ: Well, this goes back to what we were saying before: that you cannot make a comparison between moral values and the

zeitgeist of the times, because such a comparison is pure chaos and can only result in superficial and/or judgmental ideas that are completely off the mark. After all, the fabric is too wide and we are too close to it. Take as an example Michelangelo and the times in which he lived, which were completely corrupt and decadent, and yet he is still expressing something that the period in which he was living did not yet see. Nonetheless, the expression is definitely happening; and so, too, Bacon, who was also out of sync with his time and also very flamboyant, was expressing very much the times in which he lived. Later, of course, these people (and Samuel Beckett is another example, although I did not know him) are seen as having formulated something fundamental that everybody else finally has more or less acknowledged as a part of current reality. As for Genet, why should I care about the fact that he was a thief at all, when, in any case, it happened thirty years ago? And his was not a very big crime, you know; he was a little thief. It is the work that Genet or Bacon has produced that has interested me, and not, in Genet's case, the fact that he committed a crime.

DI PIETRO: I was wondering if you acquired those paintings in that month before Francis Bacon died.

BOULEZ: Yes, I acquired them right before he died. I met Bacon through a mutual friend who was, in fact, interviewing him and brought us together to meet. So this was late in life, although I saw Bacon once a long time ago when I was in London for *Pelleas et Melisande.* A friend of mine invited me for dinner on Christmas Day, and we spoke but then I did not see him for many years because you know life is like that. After when I came back to Paris, this friend brought us together and that was when he dedicated these paintings to me. Just one month before his death he went to the concert where I played *Explosante-Fixe*

and was very pleased with that work, and he created those paintings, and then I read after that that he died.

With Bacon and many other artists including Giacometti, I tried to interest these artists—many of whom I felt close to, in any case—in music. For example, there is a funny story concerning Giacometti, who I used to know through Stravinsky, who was quite fond of him. And so, when I was making a recording of Stravinsky's *Agon*, I asked Giacometti if he had any drawings for the cover of the LP. Giacometti said he would think about it and in two weeks we would get together. Very shortly after that, we met in a café and he pulled out of his pocket a handful of recent drawings he had been doing of apples, saying, "Would these do for the Stravinsky work?" [Laughs] I told him that "really we cannot do apples for the cover of *Agon*," but knowing that he had done Stravinsky's portrait, I asked him for that, and so the portrait appeared on the cover of the LP. But when he brought me the drawings with apples on them, that was so funny, I must say, and I have one at home. Giacometti gave it to me—the original, yes.

I liked very much when I was young to have contact with all these people; now I have, unfortunately, not much time left, but that was very interesting to have this kind of community interested in music. Masson was another who was interested in music. Miro, less, but he *was*, through personal sympathy. So I had quite a lot of painters doing all these covers, and it was fun.

DI PIETRO: Are you familiar with any other contemporary painters?

BOULEZ: Well, yes, of course. I am not familiar with all the recent developments. I don't have time, certainly, to go see them. But especially up until 1958 before I left for Germany, I was rather directly interested because I had more time to go to galleries in this period.

DI PIETRO: What artists in that time frame were you sympathetic to?

BOULEZ: Well, you know, the two people who were the most striking for me, I met in New York when I was there for the first time in 1952. They were DeKooning and Pollack. Unfortunately, Pollack was completely drunk, so it was a very chaotic conversation because his nose was on the table, practically. With DeKooning, it was different because I went to his *atelier* and was looking at all the series of women he did at that time, in this period. For me it was very striking. I liked very much to be confronted with all these people. Unfortunately, most of the painters or artists are not really interested in music. We tried at the Pompidou Centre to have musicians and artists have a dialogue and maybe have a project or not, but just to exchange ideas—because not a single figure in the plastic arts comes to our concerts at Ircam.

DI PIETRO: I suppose, depending on which time period one is talking about and which city one is discussing, that's not unusual. It has not been the case with New York, for example.

BOULEZ: No, I suppose not, but even in the previous generation it was like that as well. I knew for instance, Miro; I knew Masson. Picasso was not at all interested in music; Matisse not much, either, although he did the suite on jazz. The man who was interested in music in Europe of that generation was Masson—Andre Masson, and Max Ernst. Today in parts of Paris among the young people in the visual arts, they are entirely absent from concert life, or you hear from time to time that they hear a little Mozart. That's very disappointing—that there is no exchange of any kind. Also, musicians do not show a great interest in the visual arts, I must say—most of them.

DI PIETRO: I'm interested in what the library of Pierre Boulez is like.

BOULEZ: My musical library or my reading library?

DI PIETRO: Your reading library.

BOULEZ: Well, there are many books, more or less in three cultures: French literature; German literature, even in translation and in the original texts; and English literature, both in translation and the original texts. I'm sorry, but all the other literature—Italian and Spanish, for example—I read in translation. It would be difficult for me to read Dante in the original; I read that in translation.

DI PIETRO: So, did you read Georges Bataille later? I once asked you about Bataille. Did you know him?

BOULEZ: I knew Bataille's work since 1945–46 when I was young. I met him once from a distance. He was giving a lecture and I went to his lecture, but I did not know him. No, he was of a completely different generation. But certainly he was very well known in France in 1945–46. Other people, like Blanchot, I've read but I've never met. On the contrary, I met DeLeuze, Foucault, Roland Barthes, Derrida. I met and read all those people. We didn't get in touch constantly because the time is very difficult to find. But certainly I knew them, and I have read their books.

DI PIETRO: When did you know Foucault, for example?

BOULEZ: Foucault and I are of the same generation, and I met him in 1951. During the later fifties we were both out of France.

At a certain point we met, and then for a period of time we did not meet at all. We were informed about each other, certainly. I read his books, but that was all. There was a kind of proximity of thinking that was very close, even without thinking about it, a kind of parallelism between our ways of thought. Later we had the opportunity of talking to each other, especially after 1976 when I returned to France.

DI PIETRO: In the English transcription of an interview you did with Foucault before his death in 1984, there seems to be a highly charged polemical environment. Yet, after careful reading, it is still not clear what the sources of this antagonism really are. At one point, it seems, you come to loggerheads on the subject of contemporary music and the public. In a variety of ways you seem to imply that Foucault is naïve about music. Yet in his biography *The Passion of Michel Foucault,* James Miller believes that—at one point, at least—you were much closer to Foucault's ideas. Eribon, Foucault's other biographer, points out that you attended his funeral. Is it possible to put into perspective, if only in summary fashion, what this dialogue was really about? Is it possible that the English transcription was mistranslated?

BOULEZ: There was no polemic in that interview—that is a misunderstanding. Foucault and I agreed to do this interview together, and we sat down and discussed how we could go about it. We each wrote out our part of the interview on the concerns that each of us held. We had in common the concern about the role of the intellectual and music, which we both agreed was very important and in need of being addressed, especially the lack of knowledge of music generally. Yet Foucault was reluctant to give himself to a full discussion of music, because he felt he did not know music sufficiently well to talk about it in depth.

I remember very well that this was the case when I organized a seminar at the College de France on the topic of time and music. I thought that time is a topic that philosophers have always been interested in, and this might be a way to elicit some interest in music. I invited Roland Barthes and Gilles DeLeuze and Foucault. Well, you can imagine there was a very large public which gathered for these three names. I remember that Barthes went on to give a brilliant and witty improvisation, but as you know, Barthes was not so much interested in contemporary music. Rather, he was fond of Schumann, especially the Schumann of the lieder. DeLeuze, however, went on to give a serious and rather vigorous series of thoughts on the problem of time and music, which was later published. Foucault, however, gave only a series of provisional remarks because, as I said, he felt he could not address music in any depth. So, to come back to the question: No, there was no polemic at all, and in fact we were more in agreement than not.

DI PIETRO: I'm wondering what your current reading is right now, in French.

BOULEZ: Right now I'm reading in translation a Russian writer, Bulgakov, who is very interesting. That's one of the men, of course, who was under Stalin. He wrote *The Master and Marguerite*—a marvelous book. There is in French now a big book of translation of his work. It is very interesting to see how the real literature was in Russia before Stalinism. It is very, very imaginative. Sometimes it's close to Kafka. He wrote a novel about a doctor who gives a dog the brain of an assistant [laughter]. I don't have the title at the moment. He is at the same time very funny and nightmarish; if you come across his work, read him—Bulgarkov.

DI PIETRO: I am curious about what an opera by Pierre Boulez would be about. I've read that you have had a number of abortive attempts. Could you tell me something about that?

BOULEZ: In the beginning, when I started to think about composing an opera, I did not want any deadlines, so I could find the right writer with which to collaborate. First, there was Genet and later, Koltes (another French writer), and then Heiner Mueller, a German. All three attempts at a collaboration ended in a very sad way. First, I had a project with Genet, but it was difficult because he was not writing much anymore. Yet, I convinced him to begin, and we had several sessions together, and then he died. Then I tried Koltes, who was a good friend of Patrice Chereau, who had put his plays on stage very successfully, and then he died. For the third, I had an acquaintance with Heiner Mueller through Daniel Barenboim in Berlin. We began to speak very seriously. We had quite a lot of meetings, and then he died also. So, I am looking for the fourth time now for a writer, who I hope will not die.

DI PIETRO: So, through all of that, you are definitely envisioning a new work for the opera?

BOULEZ: Yes, yes, I have very precise ideas. Especially when I had discussions with Genet and Mueller, I told them that I wanted a special relationship between the music and the theatre. Yet, I don't want to say outright, "Write something for me on this subject"—certainly not, because they have their own invention. Then, there is the fact that I have quite a lot of experience with music theater, although I haven't conducted all that many operas. What I have done has been substantial in quite differing repertoire. I've done Wagner's *Ring* and *Parsifal* as well as Debussy's *Pelleas et Melisande*. I've done the two Berg operas, *Wozzeck* and *Lulu*, and

I have done Schoenberg's *Moses und Aron,* and all with Chereau
and Peter Stein—people who are exciting from the stage point of
view. So, I know very well what I want to do, especially since I go
to the theater quite often when I have the time, because theater
has always been of great importance to me. I am also very interested in the tradition of Japanese theater, like the Noh and Bun-
raku, which I find extremely interesting. In fact, I would like to
renovate the theater in this direction. I tried to do that with my
work *Répons,* which cannot be performed in a conventional concert hall because of the setting. I would also very much like to
change the relationship between instruments and voices in opera
using technology to try to have an equivalent of masks in sound. By
that I mean I would have voices with a sound mask and instruments with a sound mask through the processing of computers. I
could, in fact, have quite a lot of things, which are difficult to realize in a conventional opera house. I think it is possible if you think
about it with a stage director—taking into consideration acoustical
problems and deciding, with the librettist from the beginning, how
to integrate those problems, since music is much less flexible than
theater. In *Répons,* I had the orchestra in the center, the audience
around the orchestra, and six soloists behind the audience with
loudspeakers and all of the sound coming from the instruments
completely transformed by technology. There were also video images that were moving, as well as the sound, which is moving, but,
I mean, it is not a baseball game! No. No.

Last, but not least, I would like to establish for the theater some
kind of topography different from the conventional stage-pit
arrangement. Of course, conventions exist not just because they
are conventional but because they are efficient, yet I hope to find
a way to integrate convention with renovations. On the level of a li-
bretto, to go back to your question, it will not be a conventional
story—that I can say quite plainly. Rather, it will be a kind of story

that exists on different levels and uses different points of view in overlapping and simultaneous configurations.

TEACHING

DI PIETRO: I've been meaning to ask you: Has there been a question you would have liked me to have asked you? Some topic that is especially close to you at the moment, that we have not talked about?

BOULEZ: About teaching maybe—we never spoke about teaching. Ah, but I will be very negative. I think teaching is impossible—simply that, from my point of view.

DI PIETRO: That's interesting, from my point of view. If I may, for a moment, I'd like to tell you that as a college teacher, I have used almost as a guiding principle your idea that the whole system ought to be rethought.

Boulez once told Delige that education should be a question of movement. The teacher should place himself on the same level as his students. He should test himself out and constantly vary his methods. He should not come into the classroom with a completely dead curriculum referring only to the past but should teach with reference to the present, and the past should be experienced in terms of the present. He should even vary the end result of his teaching and try to advance as he goes along.

Everything finally comes "to be seen in terms of examinations—a sort of police investigation into your ability to carry out one sort of

work or another. Unless one combines education with experiment and invention, the result will be a total incapability of expression."

Boulez went on to say that very few people possess the desire to exist independently strongly enough to feel forced to alter the patterns of their lives and to reexamine themselves. Even from a professional point of view, it would be very difficult to require this of everyone.

DI PIETRO: I can tell you that here in the States, your "credo" on teaching can be carried out at the bottom of the educational system (as an adjunct like myself, because no one cares about what I do except my students, of course), or you can have a similar freedom at the very top of the pyramid. It is in the middle ground of college teaching that you find the vast panoply of what's left of the tenured stasis, where movement, putting yourself on the level of your students and experiment, is very difficult indeed. Not that this is a hard and fast rule, by any means, but colleagues in the middle ground often complain bitterly to me of the high price of security. Sometimes they look at me with a brief if short-lived envy, since I've taken the miserably paid road scholar situation and turned it into the raison d'être of teaching while retaining my freedom. How do you feel about this "credo" on teaching twenty years later, and what about your courses at the College de France?

BOULEZ: First, I must say that I think exactly the same way, and as I may have told you, I am not a born teacher at all! I like the experience of teaching from time to time, when I have something to communicate on specific things. Generally, my teaching job is to conduct an orchestra. That is where I teach the members of the orchestra the works I like. That is a teaching which I like because you have the flesh of the music and not only the bones of the music. So I have not had that much experience teaching and cer-

tainly have not had the experiences you have just described. Early on there were courses I gave at Darmstadt and later at Basel. Then at the College de France things were on a completely different level. The purpose of the College de France is to inform your audience of what you are doing or searching for in your work at the present time. There is no specific class in a required topic, for instance. It is simply to communicate what you are doing. My seminars were always on the problems I met or encountered in the course of my work. For instance, I had chosen in my last year's lecture the topic "The Work without an End." The question, more specifically, was the possibility or impossibility of having a work closed or, on the contrary, to have a work open—which means examining various transformations until you are able to ask questions about what is the actual ending of a work. This is, of course, a subject which is very interesting to me.

In other years, I gave seminars on topics like automatism, periodicity, and freedom. I chose that subject because I was at that time composing *Répons* or *Explosante-Fixe*. So that is not at all the same kind of teaching as, say, a composition teacher or a teacher with your varied experiences. As a composition teacher, you need to do analysis of some kind (at least the way I conceive of it). You have to show how to take something from the work at hand and then to transform it into something personal. You are obliged to cover certain works. If, for instance, like Messiaen, you stay for thirty years as a professor of composition, you cannot go for ten years without speaking about *Tristan*. You cannot go for fifteen years without going back to the string quartets by Beethoven, and so on and so forth. So, it was a choice I made when I left Basel, in which I said I don't want to teach composition. I will perform and from time to time give classes. Now this is not to say that I do not admire very much the resourcefulness you have spoken of to teach, because that is very much a special gift, and this gift I don't have.

Now to come back to why teaching is impossible for me. I think one can orient someone with analysis and analyzing pieces; that can be an incentive toward the development of the student. But composition, I think, is very difficult to teach—maybe quite practically impossible to teach because of what you can make the student aware of, say, to deduce, as much as possible from a musical idea. But how this makes the ideas work together one after the other will be very difficult to teach, indeed.

Apart from that, I don't see what you can say. You can control, for instance, mechanical aspects, such as a chord is not well written, so you can teach more control about what you are writing. You can teach instrumentation; you can say this will not be balanced or this is not right and so on and so forth. But as for invention? How can you teach that? For me, that's the big problem in composition. Therefore, some marvelous composers—and this applies also to other teaching—some extraordinary violinists have taught no students, of any brilliance, and some very modest teachers have had wonderful students. You don't know why exactly? For me, it remains a mystery.

DI PIETRO: I remember when Francis Bacon made the remark when he was asked, "Did you go to art school?" He said, "No, thank God, I would have been taught all the things I don't want to know." [General laughter] I wouldn't go that far, would you?

BOULEZ: No, because you have to know a couple of things; besides, you cannot be a mason without knowing what the cement is, what the brick is, and so on and so forth, in order to build a house. You have to know the material, and that's essential. The kind of "mechanical aspects"—that you can learn and teach, but apart from that, beyond that, I don't see what you can do (what can be taught). This for me is always puzzling about the teaching of com-

position. Therefore, I don't think I will have a legacy from this point of view—a legacy to have students, or people around me—because I am embarrassed by that. I understand, for instance, on the contrary, when I meet younger composers, I would rather play them—that will be much more interesting—than if I give advice. I say, "I'll play the work, so look and listen and learn, because you can learn only from experience." When I was in *conservatoire*, there was nothing at all between the class where you were learning how to write music and the classes in composition. No contact whatsoever between them, and I found that not good at all. So the only way . . . as you can only really learn to conduct when you are conducting, so you can only really learn to compose when you compose and you listen to what you have done. For me that's the only way.

DI PIETRO: In a way, you agree with Stravinsky, who said almost the same thing when he warned young composers about the hazards of university teaching and education?

BOULEZ: Yes, well, with education, if you want to know the history of music, for example—myself, I never studied musicology at all, but I was interested as a conductor to put composers in their surroundings. If you look at Bach, you don't look at him in the same way if you know what was going on in the eighteenth century. That's different than just ignoring these things (the time and place of a composer) or not knowing all the details about the period. You must have at least some knowledge—an impression, say, of what was the literature of the time, and the art of the time, even if it not absolutely parallel. At least you have a notion of what was going on in this period. That's very important. I find musicians who don't have this minimum of culture have a difficult time in bringing out the mentality of the work at hand which should be there, after all.

3

THE NEW BOULEZ: RECENT WORKS WITH COMPUTERS

DI PIETRO: The new recordings of *Répons, Explosante-Fixe, Sur Incises,* and *Anthèmes II* are finally out. I note that *Répons* and *Explosante-Fixe* have changed many times since the seventies and early eighties. Could you speak about their evolution and your involvement in electronic music in general? How has that changed over the years?

BOULEZ: Well, of course in the beginning, my experiences with electronic music were fraught with difficulties. I had rather bad experiences with the medium of tape music, and listening to loudspeakers in general was not at all satisfactory. But what was really restrictive from my point of view was the idea of the performer following the tape in a kind of straitjacket, which I found to be very detrimental to the performance in general. It was because of this that I pushed research at Ircam toward live electronics, live computer systems, and real-time situations. In this way I wanted the "electronic element" (which over the years had evolved to the use of computers) to be geared toward the concert situation.

I also wanted to make the language of computer programming much more intuitive for the composer. Before it was very cumbersome, with many figures and decibels and so on, and then there was the long wait before the computations were finished, as much as a half hour or more. This was completely discouraging because the musician does not think in terms of hertz, of course, which is fine for the engineer. So I wanted to find a way to have a language which speaks clearly to the intuition of a composer, where you could make sketches rapidly, on the spot, even.

DI PIETRO: I remember once that you spoke of these same problems, but how did this affect *Répons* and *Explosante-Fixe*?

BOULEZ: Well, I started and stopped both *Répons* and *Explosante-Fixe* many times depending on the technology that was available. Gradually I moved to the midi-piano and midi-flute and later still to the "score follower," where the computer follows the score which you then can have act as a triggering mechanism within the performance. Later still I linked the instrumentalist and the score to a third aspect, called an "artificial score." Here the computer reads the data of the performer's performance to modify the artificial score and have an interaction between the player and the machine, as in the violin part interacting with the computer in *Anthèmes II*. All of that would take a very long time to explain in any detail.

DI PIETRO: I am wondering if the further projected expansions of these works will be coming any time soon? Sometimes I feel there is an aspect to Boulez like Schoenberg; where it might not be necessary to carry out all the permutations of a cycle.

BOULEZ: Well, for example with *Explosante-Fixe*, I am not in a hurry to complete the other projected parts. As it is, the three parts

are very well linked to each other, and if there are more of them, they will be added to an even bigger form.

As for *Répons*, where I progressively added elements, you are in the midst of a spiral form. Even if you add new sections, it does not change the fact that it is still a spiral; you only have to mark the beginning and end of this process, so in a sense it does not matter where you stop. I am very fond of this type of form that is infinite, with its double meaning, which can be extended indefinitely.

DI PIETRO: So, in a sense, once a certain amount of the material has been completed (committed to paper and performed), you are in a trajectory of the long *durée*. At some point along this infinite spiral, it may not matter if the work materializes, like Schoenberg? For in these works one gets the impression of a seamless landscape, of Braudelian panoramas and vistas.

BOULEZ: Yes.

DI PIETRO: Just when you think Boulez is about to reveal himself, the entire perspective shifts right out from under you, in a seamless way. It's accessible—it's not accessible; it's revealing—it's not revealing. And then there are echoes or reminiscences—very briefly, from any number of composers of the past and present, but very subtle, fully absorbed. Am I right about this absorption, for example?

BOULEZ: Yes, for me you can have influences and actually you cannot live without influences, but they have to be absorbed in principle. For me you have to go to the core of what pushed the composer to write in the first place. Then you can use what you have discovered, but not stylistically.

My last piece, *Sur Incises*—for three pianos, three harps, and three percussion—is a continuous work because I want to have more and more of these vistas or panoramas, as you called them— actually a long trajectory (like *Répons,* which is also about forty-five minutes). I want to get rid of the idea of compartments in a work— once again, similar to Proust, where you find that the narration is continuous. You have, of course, chapters in Proust, but the work has to be read in one go. That for me is one of my main goals in music (for large works). I don't want any breaks in the music, but you can introduce new ideas and abandon some other ideas, like the characters in a novel.

DI PIETRO: Is this happening also in *Anthèmes I & II*?

BOULEZ: Yes, in both *Anthèmes* there are strophes, but the ideas are always coming back in a different order. That's what I call a "mosaic type form," which happens also in *Explosante-Fixe.* Ideas come back, but you never can foresee when they come back. That's a dialectic between recognition and the impossibility of foreseeing the recognition, as happens in *Répons* with the spiral form I mentioned before. Here, the musical ideas are enriched by what they have encountered. It's always the same form or arch with changing combinations or mosaics.

DI PIETRO: Could you tell me how that happens with the violin of *Anthèmes II* and the electronics?

BOULEZ: Well, the electronics have nothing to do with the form. It has to do with the motives played by the violin. It would take too long to explain this in its entirety, how it is conceived. I have the same type of development of ideas, but sometimes with the violin and sometimes with the electronics. For instance, when there is

some action on the violin, when it is prolonged by some electronic device, let's say sampling and so on, you can have pizzicatti which are very irregular in the violin and which are accompanied by samplings of pizzicatti in the computer, but completely aleatoric. Then you have a mixture of the aleatoric and written-down values, which is very interesting because it is completely unforeseeable.

DI PIETRO: So you have programmed the machine to follow the violin?

BOULEZ: Yes, the machine is programmed to play a certain number of pitches which are the same pitches that the violin plays, yet those pitches are totally aleatoric as they appear, but that does not mean that you cannot choose a field. You can make some pitches appear more frequently than other ones. You can orient the aleatoric process.

DI PIETRO: Have you experimented with the machine actually interpreting the sounds?

BOULEZ: No, that is precisely the difference between the machine and the human being, because the performer has a gesture which is impossible to quantify. The quantities are each time different. So even if you have musical values—for example, the fact that you have an accent, or a crescendo or a gesture, that you want to present—these values are constantly augmented or shortened in a very tiny way. This kind of change of quantities is what makes the performance. With the machine you cannot do that, although you might do it artificially, but it sounds artificial. If you ask, for instance, for a kind of aleatoric process on the accentuation, you can have that, but that's not a full, real gesture—it's a kind of aleatoric gesture only. The gesture of the performer is directed toward something, and the machine, on the contrary, is not.

Manuscript score to Anthemes II (for violin and computer applications)

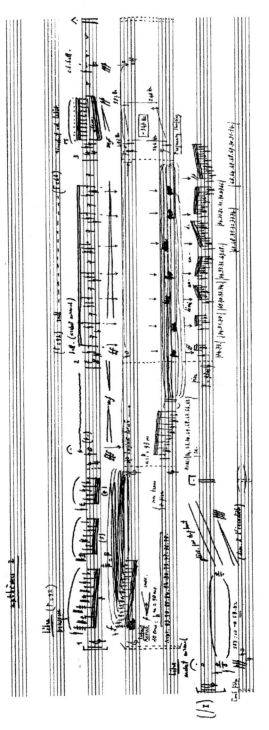

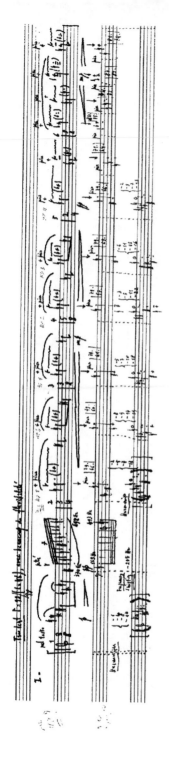

Manuscript score to Anthemes II (for violin and computer applications)

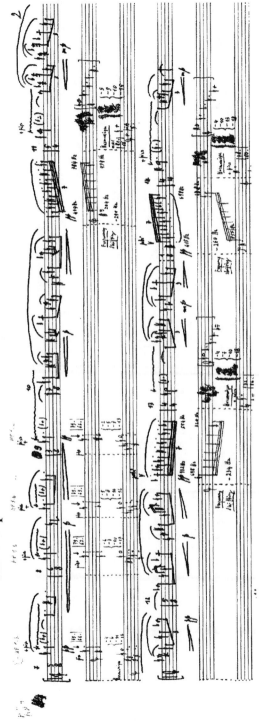

15
16
ff 466 Hz
784 Hz
mf
466 Hz
Frequency Shifting
- 318 Hz
Harmonizer
Libre
(I/II)
pos. nat.
783 : 10 → 78 Hz

With the machine you can quantify very precisely, but it has no gesture in itself. You can make (from the quantity point of view) things which are much more complicated than the performer will ever be able to do. I notice that there are some things you cannot do, with the machine, not only in terms of values but in terms of intervals. For instance, with the violin you cannot really do very small intervals (because the fingers are too thick—simply that). When you do that electronically, you hear that very, very clearly. So, you are able to grasp things that you are not able to do with our half-tone instruments. Yet you can do that with an electronic instrument. If you are organizing the pitch in such a way with a conventional keyboard, then you can play whatever you want, and you will have the pitch, very defined and impossible to make on our half-tone instruments. So that is interesting. What I call the electronics are really what I call "transgression." You can transgress the limits of what we can do with our traditional instruments now, and we also are finding new possibilities of performance. For instance, you can transgress with this new piece of mine for violin. I have some segments which are artificial sequences, which are triggered by the violin itself. And the pizzicatti are at such speeds that you cannot do that with the fingers, yet you can very well hear it, because the computer is doing it. That's interesting—to transgress the limits of the instrument with the technology which is at our disposal today.

The same with the ideas of space. With the violin, when you play, it projects because you are really there. But if you add what I call the "virtual score"—a score which is electronic—then you can have the division (sound projection) in space very easily, and instantly, you hear a sound here, you hear it there. This would be completely impossible under ordinary circumstances. Even if you actually set up multiple live violins separated in space with music stands, the reaction time will never be as quick as the virtual score. The reaction time of a live performer is limited.

DI PIETRO: So there are triggering mechanisms?

BOULEZ: Yes, we have what we call now the "score follower." You inscribe the score in the computer, and then each time the live performance is followed mostly by the electronics. Then at some points it triggers the music. Sometimes the score follower does not rely only on the pitch. It relies sometimes on the duration or on the attack. Because with the violin you have (unlike a keyboard) the definition of the sound very precise. The performer must find the pitch, but on the keyboard it is very direct and goes into the machine. On the violin you have different fingerings, and that's much less easy sometimes to pick up the pitch of the violin with the score follower. So you have to rely on the other dimensions of the sound, which are not only the pitch but the dynamic profile or the duration.

If you decide, for instance, that the sound duration is more than four seconds of a segment, then it will trigger something, and if it is shorter than four seconds, then it will not trigger. You can decide according to various parameters. It does not at all have to be centered on the pitch itself. So you have various methods of approach and the characteristics are very vast.

DI PIETRO: Is the Dx7 used with the score follower?

BOULEZ: No, we don't use the Dx7 with the score follower; the score is inscribed with a midi-convention.

DI PIETRO: You have said that institutes like Ircam are plagued by people who think they are doing something marvelous just by playing around with the technology. You went on to say it is much more difficult to invent a dialectical exchange, which is what you have been talking about.

BOULEZ: Yes, that is exactly what we have been talking about, because it is so easy to play with machines and have a kind of result which is not at all conceived properly. Because a composer may not have looked at the real relationship you can have between the invention of music and the tool that you are using; that's much more important than to just play with all this equipment like a toy.

DI PIETRO: Could you tell me how your other works are coming along—*Notations,* for example?

BOULEZ: *Notations No. 7* is finished and was just performed in Chicago, and I finished this big, long piece for nine musicians called *Sur Incises.* I have finished also *Anthèmes I & II,* so I have composed quite a lot within this year. So now I will go on with the rest of *Notations.*

DI PIETRO: The extensive planning of a new opera and the simultaneous composing and realization of three or four new works; the acceptance of a new series of contemporary-music chamber concerts in Chicago; your usual round of guest conducting and recording contracts—all of this indicates that you are in an extremely productive and fertile period for a man of any age, and, for a man of seventy-five, this is quite remarkable. The last time we spoke, you said *Notations No. 7* was "in the oven." How is the rest of *Notations* coming along?

BOULEZ: Thank you. I can give you an update if you like. As I said, *Notations No. 7* is now finished, and I am working on *Notations No. 6,* which will be finished very soon. I am expanding and orchestrating the *Notations* from particello form. Then, I will expand and orchestrate *Notations No. 5* and *8,* so that the second set,

5 through 8, will be finished and, after that, the third set, numbers 9 to 12, completing the cycle. These are difficult works, and I prefer to present them progressively, in piecemeal fashion, because of the rehearsal schedule for the musicians, so I am taking my time, especially in Chicago. Here in Cleveland, we have five rehearsals—four first general, but in Chicago you have three first general rehearsals, which is extremely short, because the contract is for eight sessions. Here in Cleveland, they perform three concerts mainly, but in Chicago you have four concerts. That is really very tough for a big, complex new work, which *Notations* will be when all twelve sections are in place. Then next year Daniel Barenboim will perform the two new *Notations* 6 and 7 in Chicago and then, after that, the complete *Notations*.

DI PIETRO: I see a number of new chamber works, some with transforming electronics, have been recently performed.

BOULEZ: Yes. I have finished a new piece called *Sur Incises*. I first wrote a short piece for piano, of about five or six minutes duration, called *Incise*. It is a longer piece for three pianos, three harps, and three percussionists. It is now forty minutes in duration. Then I recently finished *Anthèmes II*, which was just performed in Germany with electronics. It is quite a long piece, more than twenty minutes long, and it follows *Anthèmes I* for violin, which was six or seven minutes long but is now also much longer.

DI PIETRO: Are these works coming out of the proliferation of the other works, the idea of the garden of which we spoke before? Do they come out of some leftover part of *Répons*, for instance?

BOULEZ: No, no. These are completely different. They are not trees! They are original plants, if you like, so that's something new!

DI PIETRO: Could you tell me about the Millennium concerts in Chicago?

BOULEZ: We are doing a new series of contemporary chamber music called the Millennium Series, in the Museum of Modern Art in Chicago on Sunday evenings. It is a three-year project that is interesting because it comes completely from the musicians of Chicago. It is their decision to keep this music going, not mine. They asked me to do these concerts, and I said yes with pleasure. I must respond because the mentality is so good!

YOUTH, COMMUNICATION, AND FAME

An interesting dialogue took place recently in *Wired* magazine between Stockhausen and three young composers. He gave them advice on what he thought they should be listening to. They wrote responses to his advice, offering their opinions on what they thought Stockhausen should be doing. The magazine printed both views, with photographs of the composers involved.

One of the young composers wrote that Stockhausen should stop making abstract, random patterns that can't be danced to and that few people listen to. The other composers were equally critical.

DI PIETRO: You have admitted an interest in the differences between generations and even welcomed them, citing your own differences with the Stravinsky of neoclassicism in Paris, circa 1946.

What would your advice or response be to these young composers? Would you attempt to reach out to them? Can the generations find a bridge?

BOULEZ: First of all, I would never try to give advice to a young person. That might be Stockhausen; it is not for me. Nor would I think that a young composer should ever take advice from me; that is no kind of wisdom at all. Also, I would not have much in common with a young person—why should I, after all? Not to misunderstand me. I am not saying there is nothing they could learn from me—not at all. Secondly, I would make no attempt to engage with people who are just scattering a lot of judgments around and rather superficially on a moral level. I do not like to be involved with people who are simply judgmental. And last, I think that the differences between a father and son are very real. Which is why there are differences between the generations in the first place, and also why there is a lot of chaos between the generations.

On the other hand, each generation has to prove itself, and it is never really without a fight that the generations assert themselves. It has been said, for example, that I booed Stravinsky. It is true we asserted ourselves—I was not the only one—against a certain domination by the Stravinsky of the neoclassical school on the Parisian scene. But then look at what Stravinsky said about Wagner when he went to Bayreuth and he was absurdly horrified by the cult of Wagner before World War I. Or look at what Wagner said about many people, or Debussy about Wagner! There is a constant need among the generations of telling the world, "I am myself, and I want to be recognized for myself and not as a follower of such and such a composer." Each time I see among young people, even now, a kind of rebellion against people of my generation, I find that that is absolutely legitimate and very similar to father and son—that is a normal reaction, if not a kind of reflex, of life itself.

DI PIETRO: So you would still not perform the neoclassical works of Stravinsky?

BOULEZ: No, I would not, although I have performed the *Symphony of Psalms*, because I find the first movement beautiful. But the rest of the work—I mean, I can hardly cut Stravinsky, but if I could, I would! [Laughs] But *Apollo* and the like, I have no interest in whatsoever.

DI PIETRO: In our last conversation, we left off with several ideas that have come out of current trends in concert music—namely, what you called "the overly simple" and "the overly pleasant." We were discussing these ideas from the point of view of authenticity and responsibility. I recently shared these thoughts with young composers at several universities who wondered, since their main concern was now communicating to an audience, if that then meant they were not being authentic or taking responsibility? Instead of addressing that, I gave them the following ideas from DeLeuze: that "creating has always been something different than communicating," that "great artists (rather than populist artists) invoke a people, and find of course that they lack a public." DeLeuze goes on to say that "these artists can only invoke a people or public, and their need for one goes to the very heart of what they are doing because art is resistance." It resists death, slavery, infamy, shame, and control. For DeLeuze, the key may be to create circuit breakers, to elude control. Obviously, this is something very different than communicating to a public. Pierre Boulez, is there anything in between?

BOULEZ: I don't think so. Once the work exists, you have to present it as well as possible, making sure that whatever organizations are involved play their part. But really you have two levels to this question, which are not at all the same thing. Let's look at it. First, you have the composers, writers, or painters who create the work according to what they are—according to what

they are thinking and feeling, and not according to some special attribute of the audience that may be before him or her. Composers, let's say, just do their own thing, so to speak; and after, it is up to the performers to try to communicate what the composers have created. If composers are obsessed with just communicating, then they will never go anywhere, because the concern to "just communicate" will ruin their personalities—that's all! They will become a kind of transit station, no more than that; and I find that there is nothing really genuine in that. They are like chameleons who want to take the color of the audience that is in front of them. They turn red with a red audience. They turn green with a green audience, and that is exactly what these people who want to communicate at all costs are doing, they want to please. There is no personal involvement, just mimicry.

DI PIETRO: So, for you, that is not taking responsibility?

BOULEZ: That's correct. Definitely not—on the contrary.

DI PIETRO: So in your own work as a composer you agree with DeLeuze?

BOULEZ: Yes, of resisting. Absolutely. I mean, it is resistance that does not always resist, to be sure. There are some works which find contact with an audience immediately, perhaps because these works are more striking, or simpler, or a little easier to understand. But that is another thing within this concept of resistance. It's the difference between a writer writing a novel or a diary. They are not the same thing. There are various levels of communication within resistance. A composer or writer can use these different levels, because a creative person has many different facets, and one should not try to reduce the creative process to just one feature. I find that

it is absolutely legitimate for a composer to write a work which is conceived for a more effective and different set of gestures, which are more evident or obvious than some others are. So, you see, there are two levels to this question.

DI PIETRO: In my own teaching, I give a course on the history of Western civilizations concert music. Here is one of the texts I am given. There you are [shows Boulez the text]. Complete with photo, right after Schoenberg, and just before Stockhausen. [General laughter] You are in the books of history. Your projects are performed, published, and recorded. You have achieved what Bataille called "significance" or recognition for your projects, and perhaps the "satisfaction" of desire that comes with recognition. Yet for Bataille there is a horror of being satisfied, of finding recognition, because desire wants more desire, which makes us human or distinguishes us from animal life, so that the satisfaction of having one's projects recognized brings emptiness.

Christian Boltanski, the French artist, put it another way when he described himself as already in the museum, which is for him a cemetery. That is, the museum is a place like the library where artists who have achieved recognition go to die, a place where everything is completely finished—"out of this life," as he put it. He implies that he prefers to be cremated, in a way, which is one of the reasons he makes much of his work so fragile—he is happy that they will disappear! He hopes by this method to touch people who are "in the life" in order to ask questions, as the raison d'être of his art. Many young composers and visual artists would be very happy to get into the cemetery of Boltanski's museum, and as quickly as possible. This is a dilemma, a paradox.

As someone who has worked within the museums of concert life, have you ever thought about it from this perspective?

BOULEZ: Yes, but that's a question I don't ask myself. I don't care for recognition as such. That's a problem on another level. When I compose, I don't compose for recognition. I compose because I have something to say, and I want to express what I have to say in the best way possible. Therefore, generally I don't accept commissions, or very rarely. If there is a commission, I never have a date imposed; if I say, "Yes," I say when I have time and the desire to do something. I find that my life is completely safe with conducting, as I have much freedom for composing. I don't really look at the practical problems as such, as far as a determining factor in the genesis of the work. For example, with *Sur Incises* for three pianos, three harps, and three percussion, that is not a combination you will find very easily. But I was eager to compose for this particular sound. Of course, I hesitated before finding this combination acceptable. I thought of the four pianos of Stravinsky's *Les Noces* and the two pianos of Bartok's *Sonata for Two Pianos and Percussion*. I did not find this combination because of these works, but I thought of these works because of the best balance I was looking for within the circumstances of the expansion of the solo piano work *Incise*. There was a project to do a piece with Pollini, a kind of concerto based on *Incise*. Finally, when I looked at the piece while I was composing it, I realized it made no sense at all for me to have a piano concerto or a principal concertante part with other combinations. The same thing happened with *Répons*. *Répons* is for a grouping that is not at all conventional; you have to have a special hall just for this piece, which is in Paris at the Cité de la musique. This same situation applies to *Rituel*. I'm talking about the lack of practical parameters at the creative level. I did not say, "Where is the hall where I can play this piece?" For me it is important to have the idea first, and then you find a way of realizing it. Therefore, it is not a question of recognition, nor is it a question of projecting yourself in a kind of future, more or less.

a historical and spiritual glut of humanity in the creative realm, concerning creative products and intellectual ideas.

We can say that various periods in history lived with a metaphor of the times, often without knowing it—for example, the eighteenth century with Newtonian physics, with its weights and balances; the nineteenth century with its Darwinian sense of evolution (or perpetual motion, or development toward some direction); the twentieth century with Einstein's relativity (as well as Ruth Benedict's anthropological/cultural relativity) and that entire club of physicists who have defined modernism for us. Morton Subotnick says that "right now our politics has shown that relativity no longer works for us as a metaphor, and so we are at a post-modernist turning point, searching for a new metaphor."

DI PIETRO: My questions are as follows: (1) What do you think the new metaphor for the twenty-first century will be? (2) Can modernism be reinvented if we are truly in a period of glut or stasis? (3) If we are in a period of glut or stasis, are we in a unique situation in Western culture in general? If all human information has come together and is available simultaneously, is a historical frame of reference (or metaphor) no longer possible, because such a frame was always simply the product of an insulated civilization (no matter how much in expansion) that believed itself to be the center of the world? And then that civilization's shamans, in this case, the nuclear physicists, come along and admit that the notion of objectivity has been an illusion, that the observer is also the observed. The dream time of the Australian aborigines has interesting similarities to the quantum theory. We can no longer assume that life in the West represents the most advanced state; in fact, other societies have made other choices, pursued other destinies. Is this the end of the world for Western man? Is Western civilization in shock, or are we simply *finally* beginning to grow up?

BOULEZ: I will begin with the last part of your question and work my way back to the beginning. Composers exist in relation to many factors not determined by themselves. The periods in which they live; the countries where they were educated; the traditions they have absorbed during their years of apprenticeship; the historical views they have been taught—all make them extremely dependent. We all think we are individuals and have created our own world, but that's absolutely not true; it's impossible. Composers can follow the cultural patterns they have been given as models, or they can rebel against what they have been taught. People are shaped by strong and coherent environments, and they will have to deal with their backgrounds all their lives, even if they are challenged by other cultures or approaches. You do not remain where you were at the beginning. I am struck by the fact that now, in Europe, every country looks for a resurgence of individuality and identity.

We again have countries that are closing in on themselves; there is not the kind of exchange that we had during the fifties and sixties. There is again a kind of unease with other cultures, and it is really a big mistake if you are not open to other cultures! When you look at what is going on in the world of politics and the rise or reemergence of nationalism—you know, nationalism has not been very kind to composers. And now we have a multiplicity of little nations fighting each other—for example, the ethnic wars in Bosnia. Perhaps it is the collapse of colonialism that has led to this rise of nationalism, because at least before, under the old conditions, things were kept in check by the two powers. With the erosion of the Cold War, all chaos has broken out, which is extremely dangerous. In general, yes, I think Lévi-Strauss may be right that we are in a unique situation. It cannot be emphasized enough that this situation, of pluralism and degrees of stasis, is itself very difficult to predict. Certainly it is

only a very superficial analysis that can be obtained from our point of view, in the middle of this perspective.

With this in mind, modernism is something that does not have to be reinvented, because it has never gone away. It is in fact embedded in this chaos of which we spoke. But I really don't like this term *modernism* at all, because, not only does it imply a postmodernism which is not really accurate; it implies a uniformity which does not exist. Take, for example, Cézanne, who may be looked at as a father of modernism: Cézanne was someone who was expressing his times but did not fit in with the impressionist aesthetic or the stereotype of the romantic artist. He was somewhat conventional and stuffy in his private life, but nonetheless he was absolutely expressing his time. On the other hand, look at Giacometti, who comes at the end of modernism and is, from this point of view, the opposite of Cézanne. Giacometti was also out of sync with his time. In his personal life, he was rather fluid and eccentric, but he is another example of someone who was completely expressing his time. Both saw things that expressed the times in which they lived—things that other people living at that time could not see, let alone accept, until much later.

So, you see, it would be very difficult to have any accuracy in saying what a new metaphor for the twenty-first century would be, although, to be sure, modernism will be a part of it. And more than that: it is very difficult to attempt even a zeitgeist of the times in which we live, let alone in the future, because we are so close to all of these concerns. In other words, without the distance necessary to reflect on what has actually taken place, I think it is impossible to know what the metaphor of the times might be. At my lecture at the Art Institute of Chicago called "Is There a Zeitgeist of the Times?" I described our zeitgeist as pure chaos, which is the impression we have from still being inside of it!

As far as postmodernism is concerned, we might look at it from the point of view of an article entitled "Time Re-Explored" from *Orientations* in which Boulez gives a more exacting and original definition of romanticism that seems to be lurking underneath modernism:

> That which is known as Romanticism was a great adventure, an audacious enterprise of the mind; it is surely not necessary that we should retain only the heroic trimmings and faded nostalgia. One often tries to reduce it to this, to slightly extravagant mannerisms, to eccentric behavior, and to showy and cheap sentimentality. We take a poor view of Romanticism if we give it such narrow dimensions although this naturally consoles us for having to live at such an inexorable time. For many of our contemporaries Romanticism represents a lost paradise in a world which has no room for feelings . . . nostalgia becomes a make-believe in the style of very bourgeois ideas. The farther it goes, the more this view of Romanticism adheres to the mannerisms of the epoch and provides a class alarmed by the contemplation and comprehension of events . . . with refuges in the face of (contemporary) reality which it sees only in the role of a devouring monster. For them Romanticism becomes the pretext and excuse for rejecting everything which unmasks its appetites and weaknesses in the everyday world.

DI PIETRO: In an interview with Jonathan Cott some years ago, you described a kind of self-protective phenomenon against what is going on right now—a certain angst—involved in trying to find a refuge in old values that are no longer relevant (a neo-neo-romantic attitude, perhaps). Are old values really irrelevant if they keep coming back? What is it about the persistence of ideas which refuse to go away, or go underground, only to reemerge later, which seems so characteristic of this period in which we live? Does this have something to do with what Lévi-Strauss called "our insatiable appetite of a public flooded with the entire spiritual output of humanity"?

BOULEZ: The first thing I don't like and find fairly discomforting and difficult to accept is this kind of refuge people take in the past. They don't really inquire about what the past can give us in a productive way. They are just preserving the past, like they would preserve a corpse or rediscover a corpse. For me, that's the main point.

People who find refuge in the past or in the so-called neoromantic . . . *neo-romantic*—what does that mean? It means simply that you don't understand the romantics, really, who were people who were always going forward. I mean, the typical example of this music is Liszt and Wagner, more than Berlioz, at some point.

And certainly, for the nineteenth-century equivalents of today's people-who-find-refuge-in-the-past, the world of Wagner was always too rude, the music of the future and not at all of a dream of the past. Also, when Wagner took over all those myths for *The Ring*, the stories were completely transformed. The tales became the myths as seen through Wagner's contemporary society. And Wagner tried—for example, in his *Meistersinger*—to imitate the style of the Middle Ages; he invented a style for that, and that's very typical. Therefore, this new kind of neoromantic or so-called neoromantic is, for me, not neo- and not romantic at all. It's nothing, from this point of view. And it is similar to the same people who are taking refuge in baroque music because I think they find kinds of patterns there which are easy to follow.

For them, that's a kind of refuge against, you know, the music of our days or our time which they cannot follow or refuse to follow. Therefore, baroque music as a "refuge" does not implement something which is a lesson to our time but simply that kind of very old thing preserved, completely embalmed and without any kind of consequence.

DI PIETRO: So could this be a false question?

BOULEZ: No, it's a very important question. Because one sees a lot of people taking refuge, it must be some kind of phenomenon. For me, I don't have exactly the same vocabulary as Lévi-Strauss, but I think that Lévi-Strauss is right. I call this century a "century of the library." We are buried in libraries. We keep everything. And I think the strong civilization is the civilization which can burn or reject or ignore. A civilization which keeps everything which it has produced is, really, a very weak civilization. And you see that in the past. The late Roman Empire was preserving everything. The Greeks were not at all. They invented. When a century is without invention (artistic, I mean). . . . In science, for instance, invention is still a constant. Scientists are not thinking of the science of the eighteenth century; scientists have to invent, or otherwise they don't survive. I am not saying that artistic values try to be values of the same nature—not at all—but simply making a comparison.

DI PIETRO: Your view of a Bauhaus-like institution like Ircam is one of positivity toward what science can do for art. This view is not shared by every one, from Baudrillard with his denunciation of the "Beaubourg effect," to a book like Georgina Born's *Rationalizing Culture,* which I gave you a copy of last time. Have you had a chance to read it?

BOULEZ: Yes. You know with Baudrillard his views are rather well known in France and in the States as well, and he is known for his pessimism, but Georgina Born I did not know. She was in Ircam for a while doing research, and after I read her book, I found that it is very biased. She pits one person against another and describes Ircam as if in a perpetually eternal fight, with people saying bad things about each other and so on. I think it was not fair at all. She exaggerated her account. Of course, you had some people with very different views and who were competing,

that's for sure, but it was never derogatory, and I found this hardly justified her use of terminology like "clans" and "tribes." She always pointed her views toward derogatory and negative comments without ever showing the positive aspects of Ircam, and you know she never came to me to discuss these judgments. Never. Of course, there was for a while (at the time she was there) people who favored real-time applications in computer music and people who were against real-time—and this goes back to the end of the seventies! I was among the ones who favored real-time, and I said that we must really look at the real-time applications because it will be the future. That was my intuition. So there was a real confrontation of ideas, to be sure, but she described that as if it was almost a personal vendetta, which was simply not the case.

DI PIETRO: You have said that "it is all one civilization," meaning Western civilization. In this way you seem to be saying (and I think in a positive way, because I think of you as being positive, compared to someone like Baudrillard, for example), you seem to be saying there is very little difference between Europe and America on some levels, at least. I tend to agree with that in a way but have a more pessimistic view, perhaps based on my studies in anthropology. I tend to see Europe and America, again on some levels, as the last argument in your own family. This could be illustrated by the shallowness of the art world with its petty rivalries between Paris and New York. Or of the music world with post-minimalist composers who don't feel "classical music" is any longer very important to them, opposed to post-serialist composers who feel they are forging ahead with computers. For me, it is obvious that we can do better than this, since it strikes me like a father and son in greedy competition for the biggest piece of the pie. Both are the prod-

ucts of big, grid-imposing predators, based on violence! For me, it is not necessary to read Chomsky in order to know this. As we speak, riots are breaking out in Seattle.

Now, some critics would say that what I have just said is the height of postmodernist thinking—for example, Janson in his book *History of Art*. Now, you, on the other hand, seem to be pointing the way to a kind of peaceful coexistence based on a kind of reciprocal respect that I found very impressive in your description of programming *Rituel* with the Japanese gagaku and *Sur Incises* with the music of Bali. To come back to my original question about the differences between American civilization and Europe, and let's say audiences in general, how far do you take that?

BOULEZ: Well, I don't find American civilization to be very different from Europe; there are the same origins. Of course, there are many specific differences, but I don't find these differences to be that big. I would say there is more of a difference between Eastern Europe and Western Europe than there is between Western Europe and North America. There is a unity of origin which makes Western Europe and America close. Of course, the colloquialisms differences are very real, but I don't find colloquialisms to be at the core of the organism, so to speak. Now, if you are speaking of audiences in music, I can say it's approximately the same between Europe and America. If you are talking about mechanisms for the transmission of culture, there are differences, to be sure. In the States you find the universities isolated; of course, that's not a new idea—we had that in Europe for many centuries, but now things are different. In France we have no campuses or universities which are closed in upon themselves; the universities are in the cities. There are connections between the orchestras, the universities, and the cities. I remember when I taught at Harvard over thirty years

ago, there was very little connection with the Boston Symphony, and this is very detrimental from the point of view of culture. So those are differences.

SCOVILLE: If I could enter in here for a moment, we have a phenomenon here in the United States where much of our information and much of the way we understand the world in terms of education, information, television, and popular culture is ahistorical. That I understand to be very different than Europe. The reason I bring it up is because on the way here, Rocco told me he has some students who are following John Zorn, who has appropriated all kinds of things from various composers. Some of these students who follow Zorn on Web pages are under the general impression that Zorn has invented all the things he has appropriated; in other words, there is a total lack of knowledge of the antecedents. Could you tell him (Boulez) about this?

DI PIETRO: What some are currently calling a "blackout of information" (in the middle of all this information) evidently contributes to the ahistorical condition John is talking about, but I'm not at all convinced it is part of the mechanisms of "high culture" Mr. Boulez was talking about. For example, young African Americans who have just discovered atonal music and ask, "Is Schoenberg the new music?" Or they discover in Zorn, Varèse, Earl Brown, and, irony of ironies, Zappa. I'm afraid, to his horror, Zorn may find that he has become the new museum. I'm not making judgments here; there is a great deal of vitality going on, and it has not been necessary to burn down any opera houses because this ahistoricity, on one level—the level I'm talking about—has made that unnecessary. Now, I think John (Scoville) views that with horror. I see it as a mutation. Is there any example of this that you know of in Europe?

BOULEZ: I don't think we have experienced what you have described in Western European culture in general, but we may be on the verge of it because of the immigrants. For example, in France, we have a very strong community of North African immigrants, and they keep their culture and their religion. Certainly, they are a very small minority right now, compared to the number of people in France, so there is not a question of balance or imbalance, but in certain parts of the country, in the southeast in Bordeaux, it is very strong. Before the war, you had a lot of immigrants coming from Italy or from Poland in the northeast of France with the mines et cetera. These people were not very well received, but they are Europeans, and after two generations they become assimilated. With the other immigrants—say, the Algerians—they don't assimilate, and it creates a kind of hostility, because of the Algerian drama of the fifties, and this drama has not found a resolution still, especially given the unsettled situation in Algeria itself. There is no continuity in all of this. It is the reverse of the nineteenth-century colonization, an anticlimax of colonization, from the European perspective. What it really means in fifty years, I do not know. Certainly, assimilation will happen. For instance, with the young people, after three generations of Algerians, the third generation does not feel that French, but when they go back to Algeria, they are very badly received because they are considered traitors to their nation, and often they no longer speak Arabic but French. Therefore, culture and assimilation are a very difficult process for these people who come from the outside. It is different from the America of the past (when immigration for some people was invited) but not so different from the America of today. So perhaps after, in the fourth generation, we will have a situation that might be comparable musically to the one you described as a "blackout of information" in the States. Interesting.

SUMMATION QUESTION

Di Pietro and Scoville prepared a summation question. Boulez has said that he is familiar with the philosopher Baudrillard and his "myth of the end" and a never-ending process. That reminded us of him, although in a very different way. So, this question summarizes his whole creative process and perhaps his outlook on life.

As we see it, the major compositional tension in the 1950s seems to have revolved around the question of aleatoric and the more traditional, controlled compositional techniques, seen most clearly stemming from the Western tradition in which a relatively precise notation leads to the goal of a relatively uniform execution. Both views have, from the composer's viewpoint, fundamentally different expectations about the performance result. Both views—or perhaps, more properly, both techniques—have been used alone or in combination by composers throughout the last half of the century. John Cage and Milton Babbit seem to be apt representatives of these contrasting views.

We submit that both views relate not only to a fundamental aesthetic position but to a fundamental conception of life that invariably defines a notion of human empowerment.

DI PIETRO/SCOVILLE: Do we, as humans, have control of our lives and thus can actively determine and interpret our existence, or are we, in fact, victims of the process of life and thus as victims we can at best hope to passively observe its process? Is life statistical or deterministic, or somehow partaking of both?

Mr. Boulez, throughout these conversations, you have often made reference to "value" either directly or indirectly. In the light of the ideas presented, would you please define your conception of human existence? What, for you, are fundamental is-

sues or guidelines which have framed your life generally and as a musician? How, if at all, do you see your works or the development of your works, either in structure or content, reflective of your fundamental belief system?

BOULEZ: I will answer in the language of physics, and I would say my belief system is like the theory of the quantum. You have a stream in flux, but within this stream many things happen which are absolutely unforeseeable. Certainly you have a goal. I was telling Di Pietro before that if I build a work, I accept the accidents, and I think that in life it is exactly the same. If you don't accept the accident, you are making your life completely sterile. You mention Babbit and Cage. In my opinion, both are wrong—because if you are only obsessed with organization, then practically you arrive at chaos, because an excess of organization in physics brings chaos. Chaos alone does not bring any order. Therefore, I have to accept the stream, which is an order, and within this stream I must accept the unforeseeable elements, which you cannot control. But I have to make the best use of them that is possible. I think that in life that's exactly the same. You have opportunities which come which will never come back, for instance, and you have to see—to judge, even—if this opportunity will serve your purpose or not. If you see that it is of no value for you, or it takes away more than it contributes to your purpose, then you have to let the accident go. For me the fundamental fact of life is deterministic with a lot of aleatoric events that one sorts through. So life is not black or white; it's gray, and if gray is condensed, all the small dots turn to black; and if it's more dispersed, then it turns to white. And that's my philosophy of life.

DI PIETRO: So it is once again the organic process we spoke of before?

BOULEZ: Absolutely. I think in composition like that: [draws a spiral]. And I think of my works in terms of a spiral. [Draws another spiral] It's exactly the same spiral. It looks finished and it isn't finished—what you called before "the myth of the end." You just have to put something—some object, let's say—to finish it, an end object to signalize, or give a signal for the end, and that's it. I take that signal [draws spiral with end object], and I bring it to an end, and this reminds me of Proust. Last year in my lectures at the College de France (1998), I was looking at the last critical edition of Proust. That's a marvelous edition because it is extraordinarily instructive from a certain point of view. For instance, the famous episode of *la madeleine* is followed in the first sketch by what is called "the pavement," which brings memories. In the final version, the episode of the *madeleine* is at the very beginning of the work. Some anecdotes, some things which happen to a character in the first version of the sketches, he transfers to a completely different character in the final version. So, it is not only simply a kind of translation in the style but also in the characters, when you have an episode, which is attached to a person, and it is attached in another moment to another person. For me that is very interesting—when you know the object but you don't know where the object will have the better view. So this critical edition of Proust was for me very interesting, very interesting.

DeLeuze, Gilles. *Negotiations*. Minneapolis, 1990.

Duffalo, Richard. *Trackings*. New York, 1989.

Eribon, Didier. *Michel Foucault*. Cambridge, Mass., 1991.

Feldman, Morton. *Essays*. Kerpen, Germany, 1985.

Ford, Andrew. *Composer to Composer*. London, 1993.

Foucault, Michel. *Essential Works*. Vol. 2, *Aesthetics*. New York, 1998.

Gardener, Howard. *Creating Mind*. New York, 1993.

Griffiths, Paul. *Boulez*. New York, 1983.

Leiris, Michel. *Nights as Day, Days as Night*. Hygiene, Colo., 1987.

Lévi-Strauss, Claude. *The View from Afar*. New York, 1984.

Lord, James. *Giacometti*. New York, 1985.

Mila, Massimo. *Maderna Musicista Europeo*. Turin, 1976.

Miller, James. *The Passion of Michel Foucault*. New York, 1993.

Rank, Otto. *Art and Artist: Creative Urge and Personality Development*. New York, 1968.

Rella, Franco. *The Myth of the Other*. Washington, D.C., 1994.

Retallack, Joan. *Musicage: Cage Muses on Words, Art, and Music*. London, 1996.

Revill, David. *The Roaring Silence: John Cage, a Life*. New York, 1992.

Rouget, Gilbert. *Music and Trance*. Chicago, 1985.

Shlain, Leonard. *Art and Physics Parallel Visions in Space, Time, and Light*. New York, 1991.

Stacy, Peter F. *Boulez and the Modern Concepts*. London, 1987.

Sylvester, David. *Interviews with Francis Bacon*. London, 1987.

Vermeil, Jean. *Conversations with Boulez the Conductor*. Portland, Ore., 1996.

INDEX